THE IN/OUT QUESTION

The In/Out Question

Why Britain should stay in the EU
and fight to make it better

Hugo Dixon

First published in March 2014 by Scampstonian Ltd

Second edition, August 2014

The right of Hugo Dixon to be identified as the author of this work has been asserted by him in accordance with the Copyright, designs and Patents Act 1988.

Also available as a Kindle Single at Amazon.co.uk

ISBN-10: 1496146670
ISBN-13: 9781496146670

Contents

Chapter One
In, Out, Shake It All About

Should Britain quit the European Union? Or should it stay? What, indeed, would quitting mean?

The British people may well get to vote on whether the UK should stay in the EU in the next few years. The Prime Minister David Cameron has promised an IN/OUT referendum by the end of 2017, assuming he is re-elected in the general election scheduled for May 2015. Labour and the Liberal Democrats have a different view. They will call an IN/OUT vote only if there's a transfer of power to Brussels – and that isn't currently on the horizon.

The hard-line eurosceptic view can be summarised in three phrases: our plight is dire; attempting to reform the EU is futile; the prospects outside are golden. My view is the opposite: our existing EU membership is valuable; we have a great chance to make it better; and all the alternatives are worse.

This short book does not attempt to hide the EU's defects. It aims to give a balanced account of the pros and cons of our EU membership. But, after weighing them up, it argues that it is strongly in Britain's interests to stay in the EU and fight to make it more competitive and less centralised. Indeed, it would be a historic error to pull out.

Our economy would suffer if we quit. Our global influence would also be diminished.

The UK now accounts for less than 1% of the world's population and less than 3% of global income (GDP). Each year that goes by, these numbers shrink a little. We will find it increasingly hard to get our voice heard on topics that affect our prosperity and wellbeing if we go it alone.

"The European Community is a practical means by which Europe can ensure the future prosperity and security of its people in a world in which there are many other powerful nations and groups of nations."

That's how Margaret Thatcher, then prime minister, put it in her famous Bruges speech in 1988. Though the speech has become a rallying cry for eurosceptics, it is actually a call for engagement with Europe – albeit with less centralisation and bureaucracy.

Later in the speech Thatcher said: *"I am the first to say that on many great issues the countries of Europe should try to speak with a single voice. I want to see us work more closely on the things we can do better together than alone. Europe is stronger when we do so, whether it be in trade, in defence or in our relations with the rest of the world. But working more closely together does not require power to be centralised in Brussels or decisions to be taken by an appointed bureaucracy."*

How ironic that some of Thatcher's heirs want to quit the EU, as the European Community is now called.

Britain does, of course, have a different history from other European nations. For example, we were not invaded for almost a thousand years, we have a common law legal tradition, Britain is an island and World War Two was less traumatic for us than most of Europe. What's more, most Britons do not really feel European.

That said, our history is interwoven with that of the rest of Europe. Even in the 21st Century, with jet travel and the internet, our position as an island on the north-west corner of the European continent helps drive our trade and travel patterns. It is no accident that nearly half our trade is with other EU countries. Nor is it any accident that the vast majority of our air travel is to other European countries. In 2012, we made 44 million plane trips to the rest of Europe, 3.4 million to North America and 8.9 million to the rest of the world.

Culturally, we are also getting closer to the rest of the EU. There are 2.2 million Brits living in the rest of the EU and 2.3 million citizens of other EU nations living in the UK. We are having relationships and children with people born elsewhere in the EU. Even Nigel Farage, the UKIP leader, is married to a German. We are also enjoying more and more continental European food – tapas, wine, pasta, Greek yoghurt, you name it. It's not surprising that young Brits, on average, are more pro-European than their parents or grandparents.

Meanwhile, most talented young Europeans speak good English. In 2010, 93% of children in secondary education in the EU were learning English compared to 23% learning French and 24% learning German. English is also the language spoken in the European Central Bank, despite Britain not using the euro. It is the main working language of the European Commission and it is spoken in the European Parliament more than German and French put together. English is becoming Europe's language.

"We British are as much heirs to the legacy of European culture as any other nation. Our links to the rest of Europe, the continent of Europe, have been the dominant factor in our history." This is Thatcher again, talking at Bruges. She went on: "Visit the great churches and cathedrals of Britain, read our literature and listen to our language: all bear witness to the cultural riches which we have drawn from Europe and other Europeans from us."

We have deep cultural connections with other parts of the world too – such as the United States and the Commonwealth. But it does not have to be an either/or choice. We can nourish our relationships around the world and stay in the EU. Both America and Australia have publicly urged us to remain in Europe. Barack Obama said in June 2014 it was "hard for me to imagine that it would be advantageous for Great Britain to be excluded from political decisions that have an enormous impact on its economic and political life." By a simple fact of geography, we are more closely tied in economic terms to the EU than to any of these other countries. We do more than three and a half times as much trade with the EU as we do with America and 30 times as much as we do with Australia.

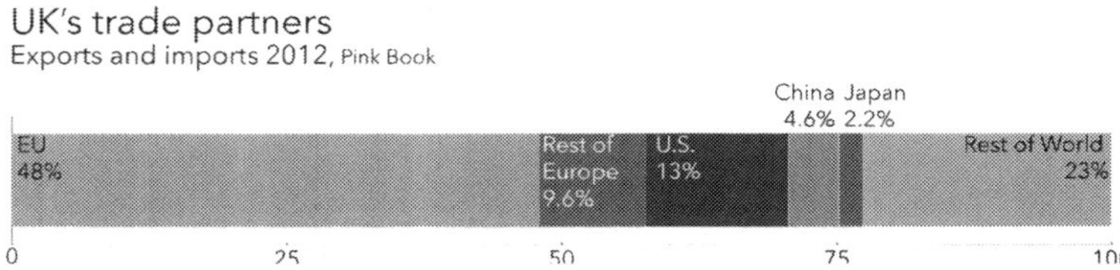

Of course, there are problems. Just to list a few: the EU's Common Agricultural Policy is a waste of money that keeps food prices higher than they would otherwise be; its regional policy splurges money on unnecessary motorways; the EU often meddles in things that are best left to nation states – such as the hours people are permitted to work and how curvy cucumbers are allowed to be; the European

Parliament seems like a travelling circus, shuttling back and forth between Brussels and Strasbourg; and EU regulations are sometimes heavy-handed.

There is also a lot that is good within the EU. First and foremost is the single market, which gives British business access to the entire EU with its 500 million consumers. Free trade is one of the most powerful ways of boosting wealth. Exports to the single market help support 4.2 million jobs, 3.1 million directly and 1.1 million indirectly, according to a 2014 study by the Centre for Economics and Business Research. We would be foolish to compromise our access to this market.

Contrary to popular belief, EU membership doesn't cost us much either. Our annual budget contribution, after taking account of money transferred back to the UK, is £8.3 billion. That's around half a percent of our GDP, or £130 per person.

When the Confederation of British Industry surveyed its members in 2013, it found overwhelming support for Britain to stay in the EU among both big and small businesses: 78% wanted to stay versus only 10% wanting to quit. Three-quarters thought leaving would have a negative impact on foreign investment in the UK. What's more, six times as many warned they would be likely to cut their own investment rather than increase it, and eight times as many thought they would employ fewer people if we left the EU.

Eurosceptics say that Britain would find it easier to trade with the rest of the world if it was no longer part of the EU. Douglas Carswell, a Tory MP, likened it to being "shackled to a corpse". It is true that if we were no longer part of the EU we would no longer be bound by its trade policy and we might be nimbler as a result.

We would also lose a lot of clout. At the moment, when we negotiate with America, China or Japan, we are doing so as part of the world's largest trade bloc which accounts for nearly 20% of world GDP. Washington, Beijing and Tokyo have to take Brussels seriously as a trade partner. If we were on our own, the balance of power would be quite different. The US economy is seven times as big as ours, the Chinese is five times as big, and Japan's is twice our size.

It is telling what a Chinese government-controlled newspaper, the *Global Times*, said about Britain when Cameron visited the country in 2013: "The Cameron administration should acknowledge that the UK is not a big power in the eyes of the Chinese. It is just an old European country apt for travel and study."

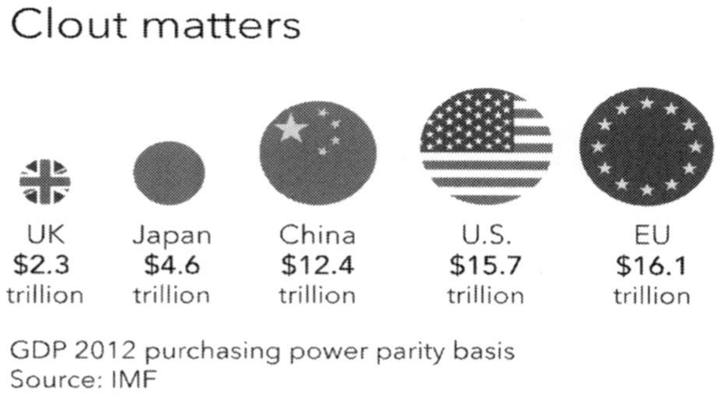

If we left the EU, we'd often find ourselves opening up our markets more to the world's big economies than they would open theirs to us. We'd typically have to play by their rules – whereas, at the moment, we influence the EU's product regulations, which then have a chance of becoming global standards. Eurosceptics say we'd still be able to cut free trade deals with places such as the US. While that's true, we might find we were bullied to do things we don't want such as get the NHS to pay more for drugs made by American companies. We'd also have to negotiate with the EU, whose economy would be six times our size after we quit. Far better to stay in the EU and use its influence to open up markets elsewhere.

Let people roam free

The single market is based on what are known as the "four freedoms". These were contained in the Treaty of Rome that set up the forerunner to the EU in 1958: the free movement of goods, services, capital and people. This is one of the most important charters for freedom the world has ever seen.

In Britain, there is little controversy over the first three freedoms. But the free movement of people is the subject of heated debate. Farage cleverly fanned people's fears of immigration during the European Parliament elections. One argument he used was that being a member of the EU meant we had an open door to 480 million people. Yes, the whole population of the EU is theoretically free to move to Britain, just as the whole population of Britain has always been free to live on the Isle of Wight or is now free to live in the Costa del Sol. But that doesn't mean that they all do. Only a tiny fraction does.

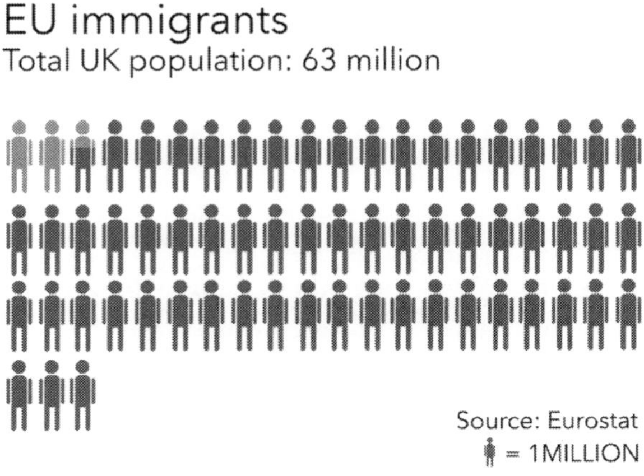

Net migration (the number of people who come to Britain minus the number who leave) rose to 212,000 in 2013 from 177,000 the previous year. The rise was the result of a sharp increase in arrivals from other EU countries such as Spain, Portugal and Italy. Unemployment in these countries has risen steeply as a result of the euro crisis so it is only natural that their citizens should seek work in places such as Britain where jobs are available.

Allowing free movement of people within the EU is unpopular with some Brits, but it has been good for our economy. It has also enriched our culture. For two thousand years, Britain has benefited from having a fairly open door to immigration. Think of the Romans, Angles, Saxons, Normans, Huguenots, Jews, Indians, Pakistanis, Nigerians, Afro-Caribbeans and countless other people who have come to our shores. We have taken some of the best things from their cultures, mixed them with our own and created something new and vibrant. EU immigration is having a similar effect. Of course, not everybody likes the idea of his or her culture being enriched in this way. But the more people experience such cross-fertilisation, the more they like it. London, for example, which is the most cosmopolitan part of the UK, was also the part least susceptible to UKIP's charms in the European Parliament elections. Meanwhile, more than half of Londoners think foreigners are good for our economy compared to just 28% of those elsewhere in the UK[1].

Free movement has also given our own citizens more opportunities to work, study and retire across the Channel. Hundreds of thousands of our citizens work in other EU countries; hundreds of thousands more have retired to sunnier climates around the Mediterranean. There are one million Brits living in Spain, 330,000 living in France, and 65,000 in Cyprus[2]. There are also 330,000 in Ireland.

If we left the EU, it is not at all clear what would happen to our citizens living and working abroad. But the best guess is that tit-for-tat would prevail. In the unlikely event that relations got really acrimonious and we kicked EU citizens out of the UK, the EU would probably retaliate and kick out our citizens too. That would be disastrous. More likely, we would just severely curtail new immigrants crossing the Channel to Britain. But if the EU then stopped Brits going to live and work there, that would still be a diminution of the freedom we currently enjoy. Some Brits living in EU countries might also be subject to "integration rules" requiring them to learn the local language. Meanwhile, if we required Romanians and Bulgarians to get visas before visiting the UK, the EU would probably respond by requiring us to get visas if we wanted to visit *anywhere* in the EU.

Now look at the EU citizens living in the UK. They come here mainly to work – indeed, 79% were in employment in 2013, according to Eurostat, the EU's statistical agency. That's not just more than the native population, where the figure is 75%. The employment rate is higher than that of EU citizens in any other EU country. Migrants both from the EU and elsewhere are also more entrepreneurial than the native population: 17% of them set up their own businesses compared to 10% of Brits[3].

What's more, most EU citizens in the UK are young and skilled: 32% of recent arrivals have university degrees compared to 21% of the native population and the average age of the European immigrant population in Britain was 34 in 2011, compared with 41 for the native population[4]. We don't pay much for the immigrants' education since they normally arrive after being educated. And, since most of them are working age, we don't pay much for their pensions or health care either. Many eventually return home, carrying good memories of the UK with them. In other words, we get a good deal from EU immigrants.

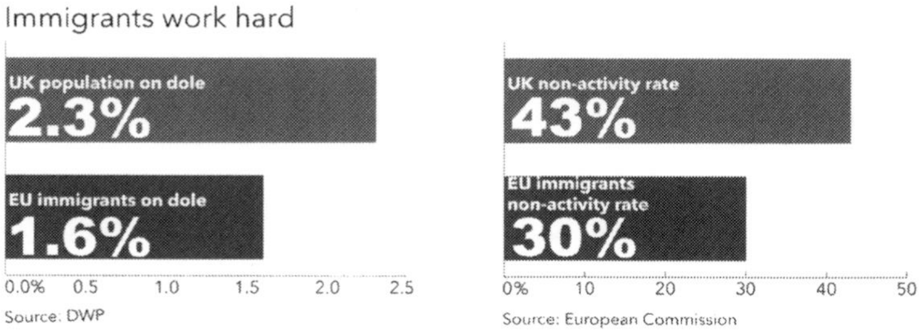

EU immigrants are split roughly equally into two groups. The first are from the "old" EU countries in western Europe such as France, Germany, Spain and Italy. These are typically better skilled and higher paid than our native population: 37% of them are managers or professionals, compared to 28% of UK-born citizens according to the Centre for Economics and Business Research[5].

The second group is from eastern European countries. Although they, too, tend to be well educated, they are poorer than the western Europeans and often work in jobs such as catering, manufacturing and construction. They come to Britain to work hard, enjoy a better standard of living and save. The Labour government estimated that between 5,000 and 13,000 migrants from these countries would come to the UK each year. This proved to be a wild underestimate. By March 2011, there were 872,000 living here.

Labour's inability to forecast migration led some eurosceptics to predict a huge influx of Romanians and Bulgarians when they were fully free to enter the UK from January 2014. The early evidence doesn't seem to have validated this.

Many Brits are also worried about EU immigrants taking our benefits and our jobs. In fact, 24% of the public think immigrants (not necessarily from the EU) come here mainly to get benefits[1]. The facts, though, don't bear this out.

European immigrants are half as likely as natives to receive state benefits or tax credits, according to a study by academics at University College London[3]. Overall, they paid £9 billion more in taxes than was spent on the public goods and services they received in 2001-2011. The native population, by contrast, paid £624 billion less in taxes than the value of the goods and services they received. In other words, EU immigrants were subsidising natives a bit even during much of the time when we ran giant fiscal deficits. As our finances come more into balance, the subsidy will probably increase.

UKIP has fanned fears that EU citizens are taking our jobs. It paid for a poster during the European Parliament elections alleging that 26 million unemployed people in the EU were after our jobs. Quite apart from the fact that Farage has found it hard to explain why he has employed his German wife as his assistant if he is so worried about foreigners taking British jobs, the notion that all these people want to work here is fanciful.

The UK economy has been good at creating jobs. In fact, 3.3 million were created net between 1997 and 2013[6]. While immigrants took most of these new jobs, 1.1 million extra jobs went to UK natives.

The hospitality industry, one of Britain's largest, is a case in point. It relies a lot on workers from the rest of the EU to run our hotels and restaurants. Many immigrants take more naturally to a service culture than Brits. If we left the EU and EU citizens were no longer allowed to work here, the hospitality industry would struggle to staff itself adequately.

Nor is there evidence that EU immigration has depressed the wages of our less skilled workers, according to a review of the academic studies by the Centre for European Reform[7]. But there is a problem of lax enforcement of our employment legislation. There have, for example, been only nine prosecutions for not paying the minimum wage[6]. Immigrant workers, who sometimes don't know their rights, are the main victims of this enforcement failure. But low-skilled natives also suffer indirectly because employers are more willing to turn to immigrants on the grounds that they are easier to exploit.

Of course, there are too many young people who are "NEETs" – not in education, employment or training – and who aren't otherwise available for work (say if they are looking after their own children). Britain has around 600,000 of these, the vast majority of whom have low educational attainments. But the solution is to train them up and encourage them to take jobs rather than live off welfare – not to prevent other EU citizens coming here. As Boris Johnson, the mayor of London, put it in 2013: "We need to help our young – not beat up on Johnny Foreigner."

Indeed, the ability of companies to employ hard-working foreigners from across the Channel is actually creating jobs because it has improved the competitiveness of British companies by helping them to expand, and by encouraging foreigners to set up businesses here too. Look, for example, at London's tech and design clusters. These vibrant new industries benefit from the cross-fertilisation of ideas brought by talented youngsters from the EU. Or look at how French entrepreneurs are quitting their country to come to Britain because of excessive taxes and an anti-business attitude at home. They often bring with them wealth and ideas to start new businesses.

No wonder Johnson has promised to roll out the red carpet for these entrepreneurs. No wonder, too, that he says: "It makes no more sense to exclude talented and legally established foreign workers than it does to exclude foreign investment."

Eurosceptics have several other arguments against free movement of people. One is that we cannot plan for the use of public services like schools and hospitals because we simply don't know how many people will come and where they will go. It is true that public services can get overloaded in parts of the country where there are high concentrations of immigrants. But the solution is for the government to give extra funds to local authorities where this is a problem, not to pull out of the EU. The last Labour government set up a fund for exactly this purpose but the coalition scrapped it.

Another criticism is that our island is just too crowded and, in particular, that free movement is adding to our housing crisis. The shortage is particularly acute at the bottom of the market. Although EU immigrants do not use publicly funded housing nearly as intensively as natives, they still make it harder for locals to find such homes[6]. Again, though, we have the ability to solve the inadequate supply of homes ourselves. We must, for example, make it easier to build homes on so-called brownfield sites like abandoned factories and contaminated petrol stations; let developers build high-rise blocks of flats in London; and discourage people from living in houses that are too big for their needs or are even left empty.

Yet another criticism of EU immigration is that it is fuelling crime. UKIP stated in its European election campaign that 7% of all crime across the 28 EU member states was caused by 240 Romanian gangs. The actual report in *The Times* said that these Romanian gangs represented 7% of all criminal networks active in Europe – which is very different, not least because lots of crime has nothing to do with gangs.

What's more, most of these Romanians are "petty criminals" engaged in pickpocketing and card crime, according to a Europol official quoted by *The Times*[8]. Meanwhile, the Italian mafia "continue to pose a more sinister threat, notably the 'Ndrangheta from Calabria, which dominates the supply of cocaine in Europe and has used its wealth and power to take over businesses and corrupt politicians," according to the report. UKIP didn't mention all that.

What the party did do was claim in its European Parliament election manifesto that "28,000 Romanians are held for crimes in London"[9]. Again, the statistic was misleading. The figure relates to a five-year period. What's more, it refers to arrests – which is different from actual convictions, and ignores the fact that some people are arrested more than once. Using UKIP's logic, one could have extrapolated from the 20 million crimes committed in England and Wales in 2009-2013 that there are 20 million criminals in the country[10]. This would be absurd.

Crime is, of course, a serious issue but there is no evidence that it is more prevalent among EU immigrants than native Brits. In December 2013, there were 4,106 EU nationals in jail in England & Wales or 5% of the prison population. That was equal to the number of EU nationals as a proportion of the total population of England & Wales[11].

What's more, we are better placed to combat cross-border crime as a result of EU initiatives such as the European Arrest Warrant. This allows those who have committed serious crimes to be extradited rapidly to the country where the crime was allegedly committed. The benefit of this was shown when Hussain Osman, a suspect in the attempted

London bombings of July 2005, was arrested in Rome and quickly returned to the UK for trial.

We should also not confuse the question of whether Britain should stay in the EU with the question of what our policy should be for taking immigrants from the rest of the world. The UK is free to decide itself, without interference from Brussels, whether to allow immigrants from India, America, Africa or the Middle East. Leaving the EU wouldn't change this.

Golden opportunity for reform

In judging the merits of EU membership, we should look at the future not just the present. In particular, can we make it more competitive and less centralised? The crisis in the euro zone and rising euro-scepticism throughout the EU mean we are well placed to do this.

This argument, it has to be admitted, is contrary to conventional wisdom. Many pundits think the euro crisis will make EU membership less attractive for Britain. One view is that the euro is such a disaster that we should get as far away as possible to avoid contamination. There's no doubt that the euro crisis damaged our economy because it was hard to grow when our main trading partner was in recession. But cutting ourselves off from our biggest trading partner would cause even more damage to our economy.

The notion that we would do better in fast-growing markets if we quit the EU is also belied by Germany's success. It sold seven times as much as we did to China in 2012, despite being in the heart of the euro zone.

A different view is that the euro zone will have to integrate further to solve its problems. Germany, France, Italy and the other countries will then act as a single bloc with the ability to dictate what happens in the EU without taking account of our interests – even on matters that are vital to us such as how the City is regulated. The notion that monetary union requires political union – with a single finance minister, harmonised taxes and jointly guaranteed government debt – is conventional wisdom embraced by eurosceptics and euro-enthusiasts alike. The only difference is that the sceptics view such a scenario as hell while, for the enthusiasts, it is heaven.

If such a scenario did materialise, it would no doubt create problems for Britain and other countries such as Sweden and Denmark that are not part of the euro zone and have no intention of joining. There would be a big risk that the euro countries would form a common position on all important matters and, hence, be in a position to dictate to the rest how the single market operates. It is, therefore, vital that the UK fights for safeguards to protect fair play in the single market if the euro zone does form a tighter bloc.

But the euro zone probably won't rush towards political and fiscal union. What's more, even though the political elites in some countries still want to push further integration, they can't agree among themselves what it would look like. And the growth of eurosceptic parties across Europe means the elites won't be able to bamboozle the people into agreeing more transfers of power to Brussels as they have done in the past. It wasn't just UKIP that topped the European Parliament polls in Britain. The Front National came first in France and Beppe Grillo's Five-star Movement came second in Italy. Political union is also unnecessary because the main problem with the periphery is one of competitiveness. Centralising power and giving hand-outs won't solve that. The solution, rather, is to restore competitiveness and boost productivity by freeing up markets. This is not a pleasant process but it is beginning to happen in places like Greece and Spain.

The peripheral countries have to solve their own problems. But the EU can help in four ways: it can complete the single market in services, which is patchy; it can open up Europe's markets to trade with other parts of the world, especially the United States and China; it can help develop a modern financial system based more on capital markets rather than banks; and it can lighten the burden of regulation on business by cutting red tape.

The euro crisis is an opportunity for Britain because all these things would be beneficial for our economy. Just think how Germany is the big winner from the single market in goods because of its prowess as a manufacturing nation. Extending it fully to services, where Britain excels, could be correspondingly beneficial for us. Or think about what would happen if the EU was less "bankcentric" and relied more on capital market instruments, such as shares and bonds, to channel funds from investors to companies. The bulk of the business would flow through the City of London with its army of investment bankers, lawyers and accountants. More trade and less red tape would help our businesses too.

The time is ripe to persuade the EU to sign up for such an agenda. Indeed, EU heads of government agreed to a plan a bit like this in June 2014, although it still needs to be sharpened up a lot. What's more, change will not happen on its own. The UK needs to build alliances to drive it. A particular low point came when Cameron was one of only two leaders to vote against the nomination of Jean-Claude Juncker as European Commission President in June 2014. Among several errors, our prime minister had relied too much on Germany's Angela Merkel to sort things out for him only to find that she abandoned him because of domestic political pressure. In future, we have to play European diplomacy much more smartly. Among other things, that means leveraging our friendships across the whole continent.

Opt-out blind alley

Some Conservatives think that the UK should negotiate a series of "opt-outs" from swathes of EU legislation that we don't like. We already have an opt-out from the single currency and don't participate in the Schengen agreement, which allows people to travel freely across most EU countries without showing a passport.

We have an opt-out from that part of the Working Time Directive which stops people working more than 48 hours a week. We also have a chance to opt out from home affairs legislation from 2014, though the coalition government wants to opt back into the European Arrest Warrant on the grounds that this will make it easier to catch and punish cross-border criminals. The UK used to have an opt-out from social legislation, too, but Tony Blair unfortunately agreed to opt in to this in a burst of euro-enthusiasm. At the margin, that has hurt business – although the damage is often exaggerated by sceptics.

Since we've negotiated opt-outs in the past, why not get some more? Wouldn't it be nice, for example, to get back our opt-out from social legislation – and decide for ourselves rules on matters such as gender equality and health and safety at work – as some Conservatives have argued?

The answer is "yes, but". Yes, it would be nice. But it would probably be impossible to negotiate such an opt-out because of the asymmetry in the process. Opting in to the so-called Social Chapter required only our government to decide it wanted to; opting out again would require all 27 other governments to agree.

That gives each of them a veto. It is hard to see France, for one, accepting such an opt-out, as it would fear British business would have less burdensome rules and so enjoy an unfair advantage.

We should also be careful what we wish for. Say other countries allowed us to opt out of a few things we don't like but said, as a quid pro quo, that *they* should be able to opt out of things they don't like. The French, for example, might decide to protect its ropey car manufacturers from competition with subsidies, so disadvantaging our competitive automotive makers. Italy might want to prop up bust airlines like Alitalia, to the detriment of our companies such as Easyjet and British Airways. Soon, the single market, the EU's most valuable creation, would be so riddled with holes that it wouldn't be worth much.

Some eurosceptics advocate blackmail as a diplomatic technique: that we should tell our partners that we will quit unless they agree to our demands. It is true that every country would probably prefer us to stay. Many, including Germany, like the way Britain has advocated free markets. It is afraid that, if we left, the EU will become more protectionist and inward looking. Others, including France, are worried that the EU would be less powerful on the world stage if the UK was no longer a member. Many of the smaller countries, and possibly even France as well, value us as a counterweight to German domination.

But blackmail will not go down well with our many friends across the Channel. Indeed, Cameron's attempt to stop Juncker becoming European Commission President went into a tailspin after he gave the impression that he was threatening to pull Britain out of the EU if he didn't get his way. We should certainly point to the rising tide of euroscepticism at home and explain that, if we cannot make the

EU more competitive and less centralised, we may not be able to win an IN/OUT referendum. But that is different from delivering an ultimatum. We may think we are putting a gun to their heads. They may conclude that we've put a gun to our own heads and invite us to pull the trigger.

A much better approach is to push for changes that are going to be to the benefit of the EU as a whole rather than side deals for us alone. This is a line that even moderately eurosceptic Conservatives, such as the Fresh Start group of MPs, are starting to adopt. Focusing on boosting the EU's competitiveness is a promising line to push.

For the same reason, it is a good idea to argue that power should be decentralised from the EU for the benefit of all countries. The complaint that Brussels meddles in things that would be best left to national governments is not just a view held in Britain. It was one of the messages of the European Parliament elections in many countries.

There are two main ways of decentralising power. One is by changing policies. A good example is the 2013 reform of the Common Fisheries Policy, an outrageous policy that led to a quarter of fish that are caught being thrown back into the sea. Under the new system, such "discards" will be virtually banned. Meanwhile, Brussels will stop micromanaging fishing policy, leaving individual countries such as Britain more power to decide with neighbouring countries how to implement measures to make sure stocks are not overfished.

Regional policy is another area where power could and should be decentralised. At present, Britain pays money to Brussels, some of which is sent right back to poorer regions in the UK such as Cornwall and west Wales. Why not let all rich countries, such as the UK, determine their own regional policy and so cut the amount of money sent to Brussels? This could be achieved without the need for any treaty change.

Many other ideas for decentralising decisions involve changing treaties so that Brussels no longer has the power to intervene in a particular area. The snag is that, to change treaties, all 28 countries have to agree. There is no chance of changing treaties unless the other governments decide they all want to sit round the table and draft a new treaty in the first place. The government should not stake everything on a big new treaty negotiation happening fast.

That said, if the treaties are reopened in a more ambitious manner, there are some reforms that we should advocate. One would be to breathe life into the "subsidiarity" principle, which is supposed to prevent the EU from meddling. This is the idea that Brussels should only take action if it can do so more effectively than a nation state can alone. Both the Commission and the European Parliament, two of the EU's main institutions, are supposed to ensure "constant respect" for the principle. Unfortunately, they do little more than pay lip service to it. We could counter this weakness by boosting the power of national parliaments to vet, reject and repeal EU legislation. Heads of government also need to keep the pressure on the Commission not to stray beyond the priorities they set it. They made a reasonable start on this task in June 2014, saying: "The Union must concentrate its action on areas where it makes a real difference. It should refrain from taking action when member states can better achieve the same objectives."[12]

But calling for power to be decentralised whenever that would be more effective does not mean that power should always be decentralised. It is in Britain's interests that the Commission is strong enough to push initiatives to complete the single market and negotiate new free trade deals with the rest of the world. We also need a Commission that can root out fraud and make sure that countries are following the rules that have been agreed to. Whenever others cheat, that's not just bad for the UK; it undermines the EU's legitimacy in the eyes of the electorate.

What's "out" anyway?

In determining whether to quit the EU, we shouldn't just look at the benefits of being in but also understand what "out" would mean. A big problem is that "out" is not a clearly specified option. If the electorate votes "out", what will that mean for our relationship with the EU? Will the people be indicating that they want to stay in the single market or that they want to pull out of it? Different eurosceptics have different views.

A simple IN/OUT referendum cannot resolve this question – leading to confusion if the people vote "out". Assuming the prime minister of the day had advocated an "in" vote, he would almost certainly have had to resign. There would be a period of wrangling while the government decided whether it wanted to stay in the single market or not. There would then be a further delay as the new prime minister tried to negotiate an exit deal with the EU. The uncertainty of this transition period would damage the economy.

But the problem with an "out" vote is not just that it would cause a few years of confusion. None of the varieties of "out" would be attractive.

Let's start with the option of staying in the single market. That may be feasible. After all, Norway has access to the single market without being in the EU. This means it isn't part of the CAP. But there is a big disadvantage: Norway has to apply all the rules of the single market without any vote on what those rules are. If Britain was in the same position, it really would be subservient to Brussels. Quite apart from the blow to our sovereignty, the rules would be written without taking account of our interests and so could easily harm us. It's hard to see how such an arrangement could be preferable to our current membership.

Norway's own prime minister, Erna Solberg, rammed home the point on a trip to Britain in early 2014, saying: "I don't think the UK with its old imperialistic way of thinking would consider joining an organisation that basically meant adopting laws and regulations that were made elsewhere and implemented directly."

Because the Norwegian option is unappealing, many eurosceptics cast around for half-way houses that give some access to the single market but without following all the EU's rules. The two main ones are Switzerland and Turkey. Unfortunately, they don't have full access to the market and they still have to follow some of the rules, without a vote on them. If we copied them, one consequence is that the financial services industry, which accounts for 10% of our economy, would lose its "passport" to offer services across the Channel.

Other eurosceptics think we should quit the single market so we don't have to follow its rules at all. We could then rely on our membership of the World Trade Organisation (WTO) to ensure access to markets. The snag is that, although the WTO has made progress in opening up trade, it has not secured anything like free trade in manufacturing – let alone services, which account for over three-quarters of our GDP. Our large car industry, for example, would have to pay 10% tariffs on exports to the EU. No wonder Ford warned in early 2014 that the UK would be "cutting off its nose to spite its face" if it quit the EU.

Investment would fall as foreign companies that invested in the UK as a launch-pad for serving the entire EU market shifted some of their activities across the Channel. Some

British companies would do the same. Unemployment would rise until wages had fallen far enough for people to price themselves back into the market.

Eurosceptics argue that our economy would get a fillip from no longer having to apply EU rules at home. But we'd still need our own regulations on employment, the environment, health and safety – and they might not be much less onerous. What's more, we'd still have to follow EU product rules if we wanted to trade with it. We could theoretically have another set of rules for the domestic market, but then our exporters would have to follow two sets of rules which would really tie them in knots. In practice, we'd probably just follow the EU's rules. We would have moved from being a rule-maker to being a rule-taker – hardly an advance for British sovereignty.

Quitting the single market would also deny our companies the chance to enjoy economies of scale which give them a competitive edge on global markets. One of the reasons Germany is so successful in global manufacturing is because it has a large home market in the EU. The ability of US companies to gain economies of scale at home is one of the reasons so many of them, from Apple to Boeing, are successful abroad. The City's success as a global financial centre is also partly explained by the fact that it is Europe's financial centre. If we lost access to the single market, we would become less not more competitive.

There are no good alternatives to membership. We should stay in the EU and put our energy into reforming it. We should fix it, not nix it.

Chapter Two
Fix It, Don't Nix It

Agenda for reform

The EU should be more competitive and less centralised. Here's a realistic agenda to achieve those goals. The ideas, which are explained in the rest of the book, are divided into top and secondary priority. They are subdivided into reforms that would ideally be implemented via treaty changes and those that don't need a treaty change. We should not stake everything on renegotiating the EU's treaties, as there may not be a quick opportunity to do so. There is a further list of things we should not do, as they would be counter-productive.

Top priority

Requiring negotiations but no new treaty

- Complete the single market. Full liberalisation of services and implementation of the rules could boost our GDP by 8.1%. *(Chapter 6, Passport for services)*
- Create an EU capital markets union. This would enhance the City as the world's financial centre. *(Chapter 4, Capital idea)*
- Negotiate ambitious trade deals with the US, China and Japan. US and Japanese deals alone could boost

our GDP by 1.3%. *(Chapter 4, The competitiveness solution)*

- Cut red tape. *(Chapter 6, War on red tape)*
- Agree with other heads of government that Juncker's nomination does not set a precedent that the European Parliament picks the European Commission president. *(Chapter 5, European Parliament: Democracy without demos)*
- Develop a more effective EU foreign policy. *(Chapter 7, Jaw-jaw)*

Secondary priority

Requiring negotiations but no new treaty

- Regional policy. Richer nations such as Britain should be responsible for their regional policy. EU budget contributions should be cut as a result. *(Chapter 7, Totally NUTS)*
- CAP. Use 2016 mid-term review to chip away at farm subsidies and direct a bigger percentage of them towards helping the environment. *(Chapter 7, CAPPING the damage)*
- Working Time Directive. Change definition of working hours so it doesn't include time people spend "on call" but not working at their workplace. *(Chapter 6, Does sleep count as work?)*

Reforms ideally implemented via treaty changes

- Slim down the European Commission so that there are a small number of senior commissioners and a larger number of junior ones. *(Chapter 5, European Commission: the eurocracy)*
- Clarification that the phrase calling for "ever closer union among the peoples of Europe" does not mean that any country is expected to hand further power

to Brussels if it does not wish to. *(Chapter 5, Who wears the pants?)*

- Single market safeguard. All legislation concerning single market should require majority of both euro zone countries and non euro zone countries. *(Chapter 4, Union or bust: the false choice)*
- Emergency brake for social and employment legislation. *(Chapter 7, Social dumping myth)*
- Green card: if half national parliaments ask Commission to repeal an existing EU law, it should be required to make an appropriate proposal. Red card: if half national parliaments vote against a new EU law, it should be struck down. *(Chapter 5, Democratic deficit)*

What not to do

- Tamper with free movement of people. *(Chapter 1, Let people roam free)*
- Argue for unilateral opt-outs or special deals for Britain. *(Chapter 1, Opt-out blind alley)*

Chapter Three
Throwing The Baby Out With The Bathwater

Say you are persuaded of the single market's benefits, but don't like all the other baggage that goes with EU membership. Why don't we just quit the EU and opt back into the single market? We could then junk the Common Agricultural Policy, the Working Time Directive, the EU's regional policies and our contributions to its budget.

Many eurosceptics would like us to believe that this will be possible. It's not. We would end up throwing out the baby with the bathwater. What's more, much of the dirty bathwater would come swooshing back anyway given that we would still need our own agricultural, regional and social policies.

To understand this, it's necessary to examine what "out" would mean. Unfortunately, there isn't a simple answer because different eurosceptics have different ideas of what sort of "out" they want. Still, there are four main options: relying on our membership of the World Trade Organisation, or copying Norway, Switzerland or Turkey. Each of them represents a different model and none is attractive.[13]

Four versions of "out"

	Market access	Non-EU trade deals	Social rules	Product rules	Membership fee	Free movement of people
WTO Third-class	EU tariff No special access for services No banking passport	DIY	No ✖	No ✖	No ✖	No ✖
Norway "Run by Europe"	Almost full access for goods, services and finance Customs hassle to check rules of origin	DIY or EFTA	Yes ✔ No vote	Yes ✔ No vote	Roughly half per head of what Britons pay	Yes ✔
Switzerland No banking passport	Access for goods Limited access for services No banking passport Customs hassle to check rules of origin	DIY or EFTA	No ✖	Yes ✔ No vote	Voluntary payments	Yes – ✔ Except Swiss people voted to apply quotas in a 2014 referendum EU may retaliate.
Turkey Second-rate customs union	Access for goods No special access for services No banking passport	Try to copy EU's deals	No ✖	Yes ✔ No vote	No ✖	No ✖

WTO membership: third-class access

If we quit the EU and don't negotiate any special deal with our former partners, we would have to rely on our WTO membership to secure access to the single market.

Advocates of this approach often point out that the EU is growing much less rapidly than other parts of the world – such as the "Brics" (Brazil, Russia, India and China). They also say that being in the EU makes it harder for us to trade with these faster-growing markets because we have shut off their imports behind the EU's tariff barriers. That artificially diverts our trade into the EU and away from other countries. A variation on the theme is that, if we quit the EU, we would regain a glorious period of trade with Commonwealth nations, many of which are now growing rapidly.

There is much that is wrong or muddled in these arguments. For a start, EU membership hasn't artificially diverted much trade away from other countries: the Treasury has estimated it diverted only 4% of trade. What's more, the EU's trade-weighted tariff barrier is 2.8%. It could and should be lower. After all, America's is 2.1%. But, in most industries, tariffs are no longer the main obstacle to trade.

EU membership does not prevent us trading with other countries. It certainly doesn't stop Germany. Its exports to China are seven times as large as ours. And even though the Brics are growing faster than the EU, that's hardly a good reason to jettison a market that is responsible for nearly half our trade. UK sales to the Brics were only 6.6% of our total exports in 2012. Even if we tripled those, that would make up for the loss of less than a third of our EU exports. The sensible strategy is not an either/or one but to trade with both the EU and the rest of the world.

It's not even clear that a Britain outside the EU would be more open to trade with the rest of the world than it is today. True, some eurosceptic free-marketeers would want us to throw open our markets to all-comers. But many companies would argue that they would then be facing unfair competition and that we should only open our markets if others opened theirs. They might even press for barriers to be raised.

Meanwhile, those dreaming that we could somehow reconstruct the trading patterns of the British Empire via the Commonwealth are being romantic. Of course, we should boost trade with Australia, Nigeria, New Zealand, Pakistan, Canada, Bangladesh and so forth. But they do not form a single trading bloc. They all have their own strategies based on maximising trade, often in their back yard. They wouldn't just open their arms and give us priority because we have quit the EU.

Australia, for one, is keen on Britain staying in the EU. Its foreign minister wrote to the British government in 2013[14] saying Australia "looks forward to seeing [the UK] continue as a leading economy and effective power. Strong, active membership of the EU contributes to this."

Finally, WTO membership would not guarantee us anything more than third-tier access to the single market. British goods would have to penetrate the EU's tariff barrier, which is still important in areas such as agriculture and cars. Even more important, our goods and services would face all the "non-tariff barriers" that we have spent years patiently removing. Non-tariff barriers are practices that make it difficult for goods and services to be sold across national frontiers. Examples include rules that cars must have brakes that conform to a specific national standard or that companies wishing to supply the government must be based in its country.

Relying solely on the WTO would be particularly damaging given that 78% of our economy is based on services and the WTO has managed to do precious little to open up trade in services, including finance.

Remember, too, that many companies invest in the UK as a launch-pad for serving the entire EU market not just the British one. We are the world's fourth largest recipient of foreign direct investment after China, America and Brazil, according to the OECD. The stock of inward investment is equal to over half our GDP, the highest among the world's biggest 10 economies. Foreign investment generates jobs; it also boosts productivity since it tends to be the most successful firms that expand abroad.

Japan made the point in its submission to our government's review of EU powers in 2013: "More than 1,300 Japanese companies have invested in the UK, as part of the single market of the EU, and have created 130,000 jobs, more than anywhere else in Europe. This fact demonstrates that the advantage of the UK as a gateway to the European market has attracted Japanese investment. The Government of Japan expects the UK to maintain this favourable role."

Hitachi, the Japanese industrial giant which has a factory in County Durham making trains, rammed home the argument. Its chief executive, Hiroaki Nakanishi, said in 2013 that he'd met David Cameron and "strongly requested" that the UK stay in the EU. He explained that he was hoping to sell trains across Europe and our government had asked him to set up the supply chain in the UK. If we left the EU, he'd have to reconsider how to manage the whole business.

Relying just on the WTO would not mean all our trade with the EU would vanish; nor that all companies based in the UK which want to serve the EU would shift their operations across the Channel. But some of the trade and some of the investment would go. That would have a negative impact on jobs and productivity. Given our flexible economy and labour market, we would eventually create new jobs. But wages would have to fall and, for a while, unemployment would rise. We would, in other words, end up poorer.

Car crash ahead?

A particular case in point is the UK car industry, which has enjoyed an astonishing revival in the last 30 years. The bad old days of British Leyland, a byword for strikes and government bailouts, have long been forgotten. Largely as a result of the Thatcherite free-market revolution, Japanese manufacturers such as Nissan and Honda have opened up factories in Britain. Meanwhile, Mini has been revived under the ownership of Germany's BMW, while Jaguar and Land Rover have been acquired by India's Tata. The big American auto groups, Ford and General Motors, are active here too.

In total, the automotive industry was responsible for £61 billion of turnover and 720,000 jobs in 2013[15].The UK made 1.6 million cars and commercial vehicles in 2012, making us the EU's fourth largest manufacturer after Germany, France and Spain.

The industry is located in the UK not just because of its flexible markets but because it is a good place from which to serve the rest of the EU. In 2013, 77% of the vehicles made here were exported. Half of those went to the EU.

If the UK no longer had access to the single market and merely relied on its WTO membership, our car industry would be exposed. The EU imposes a 10% tariff on imported cars and a 5% tariff on imported components. If our industry had to pay such a tax, it would be hard-pressed to compete. Manufacturers would shift part or all of their production inside the EU so they didn't have to pay the tax.

The switch wouldn't happen overnight because you can't just lift up a factory and cart it across the Channel. But whenever manufacturers had spare capacity inside the EU, they would use it instead of their UK factories. And whenever they decided to make new investments, they would focus those elsewhere. No wonder that Nissan, Britain's biggest car-maker, said in 2013 that it was "very important" that the UK stayed in the single market and that if it left it would "need to reconsider our strategy and our investment". What's more, 92% of automotive companies said it was more beneficial to their business for the UK to stay in the EU, according to a survey by their trade association[15]. Only 3% wanted to quit.

Norwegian model: "run by Europe"

Norway is not part of the EU but it has access to the single market. It gets this by virtue of its membership of the European Economic Area (EEA). Isn't this just what we should be looking for? Sadly not.

The Scandinavian country gains only one significant benefit from being in the EEA but not the EU: it is not part of the CAP. Even that comes with stings in the tail. For a start, it subsidises its own farmers generously. Meanwhile, Norwegian agricultural exports to the EU are subject to tariffs and EU health rules. What's more, in 2005, the EU imposed punitive tariffs on imported Norwegian salmon on the grounds that it was being dumped in the single market.

Norway hasn't managed to throw out much other bathwater. As a price of access to the single market, it has to follow the EU's social and product rules, including bugbears such as the Working Time Directive. This bathwater is even dirtier because Norway doesn't get to vote on what those rules are. In the old days before the internet, whenever the EU agreed new legislation, it was just faxed over to Oslo for it to copy. What's more, Norway still pays the EU an annual fee that is roughly half as much per person as what we pay.

"If you want to run Europe, you must be in Europe. If you want to be run by Europe, feel free to join Norway in the European Economic Area," Nikolai Astrup, a Norwegian Conservative MP, told the UK's Confederation of British Industry in 2013.[16]

Norway isn't part of the EU's customs union. That creates two further problems. First, Norway lacks clout in its trade negotiations with the rest of the world. Second, its exports to the EU have to go through customs controls to check that goods from outside the EEA aren't entering the EU through the back door. It could not, for example, just import a car from China and then export it to Germany without facing a tariff.

But what if a Norwegian-based company took some components from China, assembled them in Oslo and then exported the finished product to the EU? What's allowed and what isn't is set out in a set of regulations called "rules of origin".

Open Europe, the free-market think tank, argues that these rules don't create too much hassle for Norway because its main exports are oil, gas and fish where there's no question of buying components from other parts of the world. They would be more of an irritation for Britain as our economy is more diverse and our supply chains are more complicated. The cost of such customs controls are about 2% of transaction values, according to the UK Treasury[17].

For those who want to stop EU immigration – and I'm not one of those – the Norwegian model isn't any good either. Oslo is committed to allow free movement of people between it and the EU.

The Norwegian model offers access to the single market without a vote on its rules. This would not be a good deal for the UK. The risk is not just that rules would be written without taking our interests into account; it is even possible that, if we are not around the table, legislation could be adopted that undermined our interests. There's an old saying: "If you're not at the table, you are on the menu."

What's more, it is likely that the EU would become less market-orientated if we were not influencing the rules. We would lose the chance to push for four big changes that would benefit Britain: a deeper single market, freer trade with the rest of the world, less red tape and an enhanced role for the City as Europe's financial centre.

Swiss option: no passport for banks

If the Norwegian model isn't good, what about the Swiss option? Switzerland is neither an EU nor an EEA member. But it has negotiated access to parts of the single market.

What's more, it doesn't adopt the EU's social rules. Hasn't it got the perfect balance?

Not so fast. For a start, Switzerland has access to only parts of the single market. A big omission is the vast majority of services, including finance. This is despite the fact that the Swiss have spent years trying to get a deal covering them. Its banks, therefore, do not enjoy a passport allowing them to offer their services anywhere in the EU. To do so, they have to locate themselves inside the EU. That's why so many of them have large operations in London.

If we adopted the Swiss option, both domestic and foreign banks based in the UK would shift parts of their operations across the Channel in order to gain access to the single market.

The Swiss government has itself acknowledged the drawback[18]: *"The existing barriers to market access place Switzerland at an economic disadvantage... Swiss financial intermediaries can only expand their EU business by way of subsidiaries in the EU, which means that Switzerland loses out in terms of jobs, value creation and tax receipts."*

The idea that Switzerland doesn't have to follow EU rules is also misleading. It doesn't have to adopt the social legislation. But, it does have to adopt the same or equivalent product regulations – and it gets no vote on what those rules are. There is also no dispute mechanism so, if it gets into a fight with the EU over whether its companies have been fairly treated, there's nothing it can do.

Regulations, for example, require that all chemical components sold in the EU are tested in the EU. That's not good for Swiss chemicals companies, especially the small ones that don't have a presence in the EU. They often rely on their customers to do the testing for them but then worry that their customers will pry into their commercial secrets[19].

What's more, Switzerland maintains its access to EU markets only insofar as it keeps up with EU regulation. When Brussels changes its rules, Switzerland loses access – until it changes its laws too. That means its companies often suffer a delay in exporting when EU rules change.

Switzerland is also required to allow immigration from the EU. Economically, this benefits Switzerland just as it does Britain. But for those who want to stop EU immigration, the Swiss option isn't a good one.

In a referendum in early 2014, the Swiss voted narrowly to cap EU immigration. The government now has until 2017 to implement the people's wishes. The problem is that the Swiss referendum violates one of its agreements with the EU. So the government somehow needs to negotiate a new deal.

It's too early to tell how things will play out but the early noises from the EU were uncompromising – to the effect that, if Switzerland wishes to interfere with the free movement of people, it will lose some of its access to the single market. The EU is acutely aware that anything it agrees with the Swiss could become a precedent for a possible divorce agreement with Britain. The timing could barely be more awkward: we may be about to launch our referendum at just the point when the Swiss conclude their deal.

Like Norway, Switzerland is not part of the EU customs union. While this gives it more flexibility in cutting trade deals with other countries, it also makes it vulnerable to being pushed around by bigger powers. Eurosceptics are fond of pointing out that Switzerland cut a free trade deal with China in 2013, something the EU has yet to do. But it is important to look at the detail of this deal. Switzerland agreed to eliminate tariffs on the vast majority of Chinese imports immediately, while China phased out tariffs on

Swiss imports over 15 years[20]. We could probably negotiate a similarly unbalanced deal with China if we quit the EU. But we'd have more clout if we worked with our EU partners.

It's true that Switzerland does not have to carry the burden of the CAP. But the flipside it that its agricultural exports to the EU face tariffs as well as having to following EU health regulations.

Meanwhile, Switzerland still ends up paying quite a lot to keep its big neighbour happy. Since 1991, it has contributed 3.7 billion (£3.1 billion) for development of eastern Europe and the Balkans, according to Open Europe. It has also funded major infrastructure projects for the EU's benefit, most notably a 15 billion (£12.6 billion) transalpine railway network which allows EU countries to transport their goods through Switzerland but doesn't do much for the Swiss themselves.

Despite all this, Switzerland gets only second-class access to the single market. The absence of a deal on services, which account for 78% of our GDP, would make this option a bad one for Britain.

Is small beautiful?

Eurosceptics often argue that being part of the EU is bad for the economy because small countries are richer than big ones. Look at Norway and Switzerland, they say. These are small countries that aren't part of the EU.

It is true that Norway and Switzerland are rich on a per capita basis. But this has nothing to do with EU membership. In Norway's case, it is because it has huge oil and gas resources. In Switzerland's case, it is because it hasn't fought a war for two centuries and has developed a lucrative business as an offshore financial centre.

In both cases, small size helps explain their wealth. For example, each Norwegian wouldn't be as rich if their hydrocarbon wealth was spread around 63 million people (the UK's population) rather than 5 million. But this doesn't mean that if you sliced a country (like the UK) into a dozen pieces, we would all become richer. The rich parts (such as London) would merely become rich countries while the poor parts (such as Northern Ireland) would become poor countries.

Eurosceptics point out that many of the world's richest economies are small. But three of the world's four poorest countries are Burundi, Eritrea and Liberia, according to the World Bank. These are all small. So you can be small and poor as well as small and rich. Meanwhile, nine of the world's 20 richest countries are in the EU. These include Luxembourg, a small country which is also the world's second richest. So you can be small, very rich and in the EU.

Turkish scenario: second-rate customs union

If the Swiss option isn't good for Britain, what about Turkey? It has a "customs union" for goods with the EU. It is not bound by the CAP, it doesn't pay fees and there is no freedom of movement of people between Turkey and the EU.

Unfortunately, there is a catch – or rather, several of them. The Turkish customs union covers only goods, not services or finance. So a Turkish-style deal would be denying us a big part of the single market. What's more, the quid pro quo of even this limited access is that Turkey has to follow the EU's rules for the production of goods – without any say on what those rules are. A pattern should be familiar by now: to the extent that a country gets access to the single market, it has to follow the EU's rules.

Turkey's customs union with the EU – a key difference from the Norwegian or Swiss models – creates further problems. It requires Turkey to align its trade policy with the EU's, seeking to cut free trade deals on goods with whomever Brussels makes deals.

The snag is that Turkey does not have any vote on which free trade deals the EU pursues and so no way of making sure they satisfy its interests. Nor do the EU's trading partners necessarily have an incentive to open their markets to Turkey, as they can simply cut deals with the EU and get access to the Turkish market by sending goods to the EU and then on to Turkey. They have often delayed several years before signing trade deals with Turkey – meaning its businesses were at the back of the queue when it came to penetrating new markets.

It is only possible to understand such a bizarre arrangement when you realise that the Turkish customs union was intended as a stepping stone to full EU membership. It is not a good solution as a step away from EU membership. It would be even worse for Britain than the Norwegian or Swiss options.

Wounding the golden goose

If we quit the EU, we would damage our most important industry – the City. The extent of the wound would depend on how we exited.

The City is not just the UK's financial capital. It is also Europe's top financial centre, accounting for 74% of the EU's foreign-exchange trading, 85% of its hedge-fund assets and half of its pension assets[21]. What's more, over 40% of foreign firms coming to the UK cite access to the EU's single market as a core reason for doing so; and around 40% of our tax take from financial services comes from international businesses operating in the UK.

The way to quit the EU and inflict the least harm on the City would be to stay in the single market – in other words, the Norwegian approach. The snag is that the rules for how the City was regulated would be determined in Brussels and we wouldn't get a vote on them. Other countries might even try to rig the rules to shift business from London to Frankfurt or Paris. This is worse than the status quo. Although the UK cannot currently veto EU financial services legislation, in practice it has only twice lost out: the main one was when Brussels decided in 2013 to cap bankers' bonuses.

The damage to the City would be particularly severe if the UK quit the single market as well as the EU – in other words, any of the Swiss, Turkish or WTO models. UK-based financial firms would no longer have a "passport", allowing them to provide services anywhere in the EU. Firms wanting to do business in the EU would then have to relocate there by setting up subsidiaries.

No wonder the British Bankers Association as well as two giant US banks, Citigroup and JPMorgan, all warned in early 2014 about the dangers of leaving the EU. Meanwhile, Goldman Sachs, the world's pre-eminent investment bank, had previously said it would move a "substantial" part of its European business across the Channel, possibly to Paris or Frankfurt, if we quit the EU[22].

British citizens wouldn't necessarily even be able to follow these jobs abroad because they would no longer have the right to work in the EU. Meanwhile, the City's competitiveness would be undermined if Britain stopped EU citizens working in the UK. While we could still let them enter, we probably wouldn't adopt such a policy since one of the main reasons eurosceptics give for quitting the EU is to stop immigration in the first place.

We wouldn't be able to jettison much financial services regulation either. We need rules to stop the system blowing up. And it makes sense to coordinate these internationally to make sure things don't fall through the cracks as they did when Lehman Brothers went bust.

If we were on our own, we would also lose influence in determining the rules of the global financial game. There would be a risk of being told what to do by America, which has its own huge financial system, and China, which wants to become a global player.

The City's ability to act as the world's financial capital, vying with New York, could be damaged. It enjoys economies of scale from being Europe's financial capital. With less scale, it would be less competitive and its ability to serve fast-growing markets in the rest of the world would be compromised. And, of course, the City would lose the chance to ride what could be a big opportunity – turning the EU from a financial system centred on banks into one based on capital markets.

Much is at stake. Financial services are responsible for nearly 10% of our economy and 12% of government revenue[23]. Various associated professions such as law and accountancy are also important.

Not surprisingly, when the CityUK, which represents Britain's financial services industry, surveyed its members in 2013, 84% said they wanted to stay in the EU. Quitting the EU would be bad for this money-spinner.

Negotiating from a position of weakness

Many eurosceptics say we are a special case. We are bigger than Norway and Switzerland, and richer than Turkey. We are, therefore, in a position to cut a better deal with the EU than any of them. Clout is important – and we certainly have more of it than Norway, Switzerland or Turkey. But the problem with this argument is that the EU has more clout than us. Its economy would be six times our size. So we wouldn't be in an equal bargaining position.

Eurosceptics are also fond of pointing out that we have a big current account deficit with the EU. It exported £267 billion to us in 2012 while we exported £222 billion to it. The other countries would, therefore, be the bigger losers if our trading relationship broke down. So if we hang tough in our negotiations, we'll get a good deal.

There are several problems with this argument. One is that it assumes the only good thing about trade is exports. But imports are beneficial too. If EU exports to the UK were artificially restricted, our consumers would be harmed. They would have to pay more when they shop and would have less choice.

An even bigger problem with the argument is that it totally ignores proportionality. Britain's exports to the EU represent 14% of our GDP. The rest of the EU's exports to Britain represent 2.5% of its GDP. Neither side would win from a trade war. But we would be hit proportionately much harder.

Who would blink in a trade war?

If we tried to play hard ball, the EU might call our bluff. Imagine a trade war in which exports on both sides dropped by a quarter. Our GDP would be knocked by 3.5%; the rest of the EU's would shrink by 0.6%. It could take the hit. We would be left reeling.

What's more, negotiations could easily be conducted in an atmosphere of ill will. Immediately after voting to leave the EU, the British people are unlikely to feel all warm and cuddly about their erstwhile partners. Our government would be under pressure to take a tough line. Meanwhile, our former partners would be feeling irritated, almost jilted. Some might urge an equally tough line to put us in our place. Although it would be in both sides' interests to conclude an agreement, bitterness could cloud the talks and result in a poor outcome for everybody.

Contrast this with the atmosphere of talks between the EU and Norway, Switzerland and Turkey. In none of these cases was the country pulling out of the EU. Admittedly, in Norway's case, the people had voted not to join and, in Switzerland's case, the government had decided to pull its application. But that's different from voting to quit. The talks were conducted in a business-like fashion. Meanwhile, in Turkey's case, the negotiations were seen as a prelude to joining the EU. So despite our greater clout, we might easily get a worse deal.

Often the same people who say we can negotiate a great deal with the EU from the outside say it is hopeless to try to reform the EU from inside. This is odd. We are more likely to maximise our negotiating strength while we are in the club than after we have just snubbed our former allies

Hefty break-up costs

Much of the discussion about whether we should be in or out of the EU focuses on which is the better end state. But, as in any divorce, we should also consider the break-up costs. As of mid-2013, the government had done no contingency planning. As of mid-2014, neither had the European Commission. That, in itself, is a worry because the costs are likely to be higher if we are unprepared.

The main cost is uncertainty about what form of access we'd have to the single market. The uncertainty could be extremely unsettling for business. If the electorate votes to quit the EU, that won't resolve the matter. The people won't have said whether they want a Norwegian, Swiss or Turkish option – or none of the above.

What's more, the prime minister of the day – probably Cameron because only the Tories are promising a referendum in the next parliament – would presumably have campaigned to stay in. He would be under great pressure to resign after losing such a strategic vote. The first item on the agenda would, therefore, probably be for the governing party to choose a new prime minister.

Once a new prime minister was in place, he or she would then have to decide which sort of relationship he wanted with the EU. There's likely to be lots of internal wrangling, with some people saying the electorate really meant to quit the single market and others saying that wasn't what was intended at all.

After a new prime minister had decided what sort of relationship he or she wanted, we would then have to notify the European Council. The Treaty on European Union spells out that we would cease to be a member two years later. In the meantime, we would seek to negotiate our exit deal. But there's no guarantee that a deal could be completed in that time and, if not, we would just have to rely on our membership of the WTO with its third-class access to the single market. What's more, we couldn't just change our mind and opt back into the EU if we got a terrible deal. Once we triggered the exit clause, Article 50 of the Lisbon Treaty, there would be no way back into the EU apart from by the unanimous consent of all other states.

Even after we quit the EU, there would be further legal and regulatory uncertainty. After all, the EU's directives are now British law. Some eurosceptics will want to trash all of them. But there would then be chaos. There would no longer be a regime ensuring that the safety of chemicals, rules labelling food products, laws giving compensation to passengers for delayed flights and so forth.

In practice, we would have to decide one by one which laws to keep, which to repeal and which to amend. That would be another time-consuming process which would tie up government and parliament for years, diverting them from other tasks.

During the long period of uncertainty, firms would wonder whether to spend money here or switch production to the EU. This would affect British firms as well as foreign ones. Many would just sit on their hands. All this would be bad for the economy.

The idea that the grass will be greener if we quit the EU is an illusion.

Chapter Four
Turning Euro Crisis To Our Advantage

Many eurosceptics think the euro crisis is a reason for Britain to quit the EU. It is actually a reason for staying. The crisis has created an excellent opportunity to reform the EU in ways that benefit us: to complete the single market; to create a trans-Atlantic free trade area; to sell the City as a solution to the euro zone's problems; and to reform regulations that hamper competitiveness.

A common view is that the euro zone is going to have to reform itself by integrating further and this will marginalise us. After all, the 18 countries that use the euro account for over 65% of the EU's population. This means they will have a so-called "qualified majority" if they act as a single bloc – allowing them to pass laws on many topics without getting the agreement of countries outside the zone.

But the premise of this argument – that the euro zone is going to integrate further and so act as a bloc – isn't solid. To see why, it is necessary to understand that the euro crisis is primarily caused by a loss of competitiveness and its solution is going to be mainly about restoring competitiveness.

The peripheral countries of the euro zone – Italy, Spain, Greece, Portugal, Cyprus and Ireland – have long had a host of problems, including: low productivity; inflexible labour markets; corruption; vested private sector interests that shut out competition; lavish publicly-funded pension schemes; bloated civil services; rampant tax evasion; and poorly functioning legal systems. France shares some of the problems too.

Before the euro's launch, these countries could just about muddle along with their different currencies – periodically devaluing the lira, peseta, drachma and so forth whenever they lost competitiveness. After joining the single currency, they lost that escape valve. But the underlying problems were masked for a decade by an unnaturally benign global economy, fuelled by artificially cheap money.

The single currency made things worse because it meant governments in the periphery, which previously had had to pay a fat premium to borrow money, got access to cheaper money too. They gorged themselves on it. Meanwhile, the one-size-fits-all monetary policy meant interest rates were not jacked up to restrain booms in places like Spain, Ireland and Greece and so wages there rose rapidly. Given that devaluation was no longer an option, it became harder to export and cheaper to import. In 2008, Spain's current account deficit was 10% of GDP and Greece's 15%.

When the credit bubble popped after Lehman Brothers went bust in 2008, investors everywhere got nervous about banks, individuals and governments that had borrowed too much money. The spotlight turned on Greece in late 2009. It didn't just have a huge current account deficit; its new government admitted that its predecessor had fiddled the figures to keep its budget deficit artificially low. When all the dirty linen was finally washed, Athens' budget deficit for 2009 was revealed to be 16% of GDP.

Ireland, Spain and Cyprus had a slightly different problem: property bubbles and rotten banking systems. Their banking crises progressively infected their governments' finances.

Once the bubble burst, there was bound to be trouble. Belts had to be tightened to bring government expenditure back into line with income; and wages had to be cut to restore competitiveness. But the way the crisis was handled made things worse: labour markets were reformed too slowly, zombie banks weren't recapitalised fast enough and fiscal policy was too austere. The net result is that unemployment in the euro zone averaged 11.6% in mid-2014 and GDP ended 2013 about 2% lower than it had been in its pre-crisis peak. Things were much worse in the problem countries.

Mind you, the UK has no reason to crow. It had some of the same problems as these peripheral countries: a housing bubble in the run-up to the crisis, a rampant banking sector that needed to be rescued and a budget deficit that hit 11.5% of GDP in 2009. We have not suffered as badly because we were not in the euro zone and, by early 2014, our economy was rebounding. But it still ended 2013 nearly 2% below its pre-crisis peak – about the same as the euro zone average. The main difference is that our unemployment in mid-2014 was only 6.6%, largely down to our flexible labour markets. Germany, which also has flexible labour markets, was doing even better with an unemployment rate of only 5.1%. This is a lesson to other European countries about the importance of cutting labour regulations.

Union or bust: the false choice

Where does the euro zone go now? The conventional wisdom is that there are two options: either it breaks apart; or it huddles closer in a full political, fiscal and banking union.

A break-up would cause havoc in financial markets. The euro zone is like Hotel California in the Eagles' song – "you can check out any time you like, but you can never leave". There is no provision for a Greece or Portugal or Italy to quit the single currency – unlike the EU, for which there is an exit clause.

If a weak country did try to leave the euro, there would therefore be endless legal disputes. What's more, even before it happened, there would be runs on banks as people tried to get their cash out in euros fearing that they would otherwise be paid back in devalued drachmas, escudos or lira. Capital controls would have to be imposed, as they were in Cyprus in 2013, tipping the economy into a deep depression.

In any case, a break-up of the euro zone is not the most likely scenario because the euro zone countries have looked over the abyss and decided they don't want to go there. The turning point occurred in July 2012 when Mario Draghi, the ECB's President, said he would do "whatever it takes to preserve the euro". This had the immediate effect of calming financial markets. The rates that Spain and Italy have to pay to borrow money fell substantially and, by early 2014, the euro zone was growing again – albeit slowly. But doesn't the euro zone still need a long-term plan to restore its economic health? Isn't that where political and fiscal union come in?

You can find countless speeches from European leaders, finance ministers, central bankers and pundits peddling this line. There are various versions of what such a union might involve but the normal list includes some or all of the following: a euro zone finance minister who has the power to vet national budgets; large transfers of money rather than just loans from rich countries to poor ones; harmonisation of tax policies; a system under which governments would guarantee each others' borrowing; and a full "banking union".

The only problem is that the people of Europe don't want this. Euroscepticism is on the rise pretty much everywhere, as the European Parliament elections showed. Even the Germans are only keen on a more integrated euro zone provided it is done on their terms – in other words, lots of discipline for wayward southerners but limited hand-outs from the northern countries. No wonder photo-montages of Germany's Angela Merkel dressed as a Nazi have appeared in Greece. No wonder, too, that most of a plan drawn up by the Commission for "Genuine Economic and Monetary Union" has been put on the shelf.

Even if the 18 euro zone governments could somehow agree on what political union would look like – and that's a massive "if" – it is hard to see them being able to foist it on their people without holding referendums on the necessary treaty changes. It's harder still to imagine all the electorates agreeing. Even the French might vote "no". After all, the eurosceptic National Front, led by Marine Le Pen, came first in the European Parliament elections.

Indeed, François Hollande is so scared of losing a referendum in advance of his bid for re-election in 2017 that he is reluctant to agree to any treaty change that might require a plebiscite before that. As a result, for the time being, the euro zone will probably muddle through without any treaty changes – or with only small ones that don't require referendums.

Anybody doubting this assessment should look at the euro zone's tortuous progress towards banking union. Peripheral countries latched onto the scheme as a way of getting richer countries to bail out their banks. But Germany and other "core" countries have baulked at that. So it now looks like only a partial banking union will be agreed. Remember, too, that banking union is just one building block of the supposed political and fiscal union – and not nearly as politically charged as some of the other blocks.

What should the UK make of this debate? Well, first, it would not be in our interests if the euro zone formed a tight political and fiscal union. If the 18 euro zone countries come together as something that even half resembles a single country, our influence will be reduced. We will have less ability to form blocking minorities in the European Council.

A key objective of British foreign policy for hundreds of years has been to stop continental Europe forming a single bloc. That's why we fought so hard to stop Spanish, then French and finally German hegemony. Margaret Thatcher was alive to the danger in her Bruges speech, saying: "Over the centuries we have fought to prevent Europe from falling under the dominance of a single power." It was, therefore, unwise of George Osborne in mid-2012 to urge the euro zone towards greater integration – talking of the "remorseless logic" of banking and fiscal union.

To be fair, Osborne eventually understood the danger of what he had advocated: that the euro zone would form a single bloc on banking issues and would so be able to dictate the rules by which the City of London, our biggest industry, operated. He, therefore, staged a vigorous rear-guard action to prevent this. The final deal involved a double majority voting system on EU banking rules. For a rule to pass, it needs to secure a majority both among those countries that are part of the banking union and among those that are not.

Although the euro zone doesn't look like it's going to charge down the direction of full political union, we should certainly prepare for that possibility. In such a scenario, we should safeguard our interests by taking the double majority we secured for banking union and extending it so that all single market legislation has to be approved by both a majority of those in the euro zone and a majority of those outside it. If the euro zone wants treaty changes to engineer further integration, this protection should be top of the list of things we want in return for giving our approval.

The competitiveness solution

If neither a break-up of the single currency nor full political union is on the cards, is there a third way? The answer is "yes": boost competitiveness, clean up the banking system and have policies to prevent further booms.

Given that the euro crisis is mainly a competitiveness crisis, it's not surprising that the main solution has to be to restore the competitiveness of peripheral countries. So far this has been achieved largely by slashing wages and squishing imports. Greek unit labour costs, which rose a third between 2000 and 2009, were expected by Eurostat to fall back 14% by end- 2013. It is a similar story in Spain, where unit labour costs were expected to end 2013 6% below their 2009 peak after rising a third in the previous nine years.

Because of restored competitiveness and because people can't afford to spend money on imports, current account deficits have also shrunk. Greece's deficit for 2014 is forecast by the European Commission to be only 2.3%of GDP, down from a peak of 15%; Spain is forecast to have a surplus of 1.4%, compared to a deficit of 10% at its peak.

There are still big problems in the euro zone, especially high youth unemployment. What's more, neither France nor Italy has fully embraced the need for reform, although there are signs of progress even there.

The way the euro zone crisis is evolving offers an opportunity for Britain. This is because we have long been calling for the EU to be made more competitive – and to build an economy based more on the free market and less on heavily-regulated welfare states. The time is now ripe to push this agenda in four specific areas: trade, services, regulation and finance.

We need a single market that is open to the world rather than a Fortress Europe. As the rest of the EU gets the importance of competitiveness, it should be easier to press for free trade deals with other parts of the world. We are already beginning to see the fruits of this.

In 2013, the EU completed a free trade deal with Canada and launched talks with America. David Cameron deserves much of the credit for the latter. An ambitious deal could boost our GDP by £10 billion, according to the Centre for Economic Policy Research[24]. It would be ironic if, after doing so much to get these talks off the ground, the UK quit the EU and wasn't in a position to benefit from the results.

There is also an important free trade deal in the works with Japan, which could eventually boost EU GDP by 0.6-0.8% according to the Commission. Assuming we'd benefit to the same extent as the EU average, the American and Japanese trade deals could increase GDP by 1.3%. Meanwhile, Cameron has called for a free trade deal between the EU and China. We will have a better chance of negotiating a balanced agreement as part of the EU than if we were on our own.

The Fortress Europe mentality hasn't vanished. So all these talks will be hard. France has already thrown something of a spanner into the US negotiations by insisting that its entertainment industry is ring-fenced. But the new euro zone zeitgeist – in particular, the realisation that action is needed to boost competitiveness and growth – makes it more likely that these talks will have a successful outcome.

Completing the single market in services is an even bigger opportunity. Services account for 70% of EU GDP. The EU is notoriously inefficient in their provision. This is a big reason why the region's GDP per head is only two-thirds of the level of the United States. Full liberalisation would increase UK GDP by 7.1%, according to the government. It's probably unrealistic to sweep away all the barriers, but completing even half the job that would be a big prize.

The new zeitgeist also means we are more likely to find allies for a big initiative in this area. In the past, we could only rely on Scandinavian and eastern European countries as well as the Netherlands. But the crisis has turned the peripheral countries, including Italy and Spain, into allies. This is because the crisis is forcing them to open up their markets at home. They now see the attraction in other countries opening up their markets too.

Again, it won't be easy. There are strong vested interests in both conservative Germany and illiberal France that will try to fight liberalisation. The French will say that national rules are needed to protect consumers from poor-quality services from abroad – even though their companies happily provide electricity, public transport and waste management in liberal Britain. Germans will argue that their apprentice system ensures youngsters are trained to become masters of crafts like plumbing, keeping quality high.

The counter-argument is that French and German consumers will benefit from choice. Not everybody wants, or can afford, the plumbing equivalent of a BMW. If Germans really provide better-quality services, they should be able to sell them as an upmarket product in other countries. But why should their consumers not be able to use cheap Polish plumbers if they prefer – or, for that matter, high-quality British accountants and lawyers?

If this economic argument doesn't bite, a political one could help sway the day. This is that Germany has been the loudest advocate of peripheral countries opening up their markets as the price of bailouts. How fair then is it to keep its markets closed? Liberalisation would encourage Germans to spend more money on services, helping drag the periphery out of recession. Isn't that better than providing more hand-outs?

As well as liberalising services, the EU needs to cut unnecessary regulations. This has long been a UK demand. Again, the crisis provides an opportunity. How can the EU afford expensive social and employment rules when it so badly needs to compete? This is precisely the message Germany and the Commission have been banging on about to peripheral economies. It is about time they took some of their own medicine.

Capital idea

The UK's final big opportunity from the euro crisis is the chance to help build a "capital markets union". We need to sell the City as part of the solution to the euro zone's problems.

The elevator pitch is that the zone's biggest challenge in coming years is to pep up its sluggish growth rate, and that will require more investment. The European Commission says 1 trillion is needed for transport, energy and telecoms networks of "EU importance" alone by 2020. The snag is that traditional sources of finance are drying up. Indebted governments need to balance their books; meanwhile many banks are shrinking because they too have to clean up their balance sheets.

But there's no need to despair. Non-bank finance – everything from bonds to shares to loans provided by entities other than banks – could come to the rescue. While the euro zone would be the main source of demand for such financial services, the UK – home to the continent's largest capital market – would be the main source of supply. A drive to complete the single capital market would be a generational opportunity for London akin to the "eurodollar revolution" from the late 1950s onwards and the explosion of activity unleashed by the Big Bang of 1986.

The chance of getting the EU to swing behind a pro-City strategy may, on the face of it, seem pie in the sky. Britain has in recent years been playing a defensive game in response to the barrage of misguided financial rules from Brussels. Many people blame financiers for the financial crisis. What's more, continental Europeans have long tended to be suspicious of financial markets. Hence, the plan by 10 EU countries (not including the UK) to apply a tax on financial transactions. Hence, too, the recent decision to cap bankers' bonuses throughout the EU, despite our objections.

The oddity about these rules is that they do not to address the main causes of the financial crisis. Trading in financial instruments wasn't the prime culprit. And while banker compensation does bear some of the blame, the solution is cock-eyed. Banks have reacted to bonus limits by pushing up fixed salaries – something which will make their finances more vulnerable when the next crisis hits. Meanwhile, the original financial transactions tax would have gummed up markets so badly, increasing the cost of capital and constricting growth, that its supporters have diluted it and are turning it into something akin to the UK's stamp duty on shares. Our government still does not like the tax's extra-territorial reach and has reserved the right to challenge it in the European Court of Justice when the full details are clear. An earlier court challenge failed on the grounds that it was premature.

Despite the headwinds, Britain has a real chance to turn things around. To do so, it must challenge the conventional script, under which old-fashioned banking is seen as good and capital markets (providing finance to companies and households through bonds and shares) bad. The truth is that Europe has had a banking crisis, not a capital markets one. Banks have lent too much money to clients who can't pay it back. Their balance sheets were too weak to start off. Now they are unable to lend to the real economy, throttling growth.

Banks are dangerous beasts. They are not well suited to provide long-term finance, as they fund themselves with deposits and other short-term money. As a result, they either don't lend long term; or, if they do, they expose themselves and taxpayers to big risks if liquidity dries up. The contrast between America and Europe is stark. In the United States, banks provide only 19% of long-term financing, according to the McKinsey Global Institute. In big European countries, they provide between 59% and 71%. The flipside is that capital markets are much less developed in Europe than America.

This is not to say that markets-based finance is perfect. Too often what goes on in the markets is murky and even scandalous. What's more, during the crisis, problems in the markets often infected the banks because the border between the two was fuzzy. So markets need to be cleaned up too.

That said, with the EU's banking system haunted by zombies, its excessive reliance on banks to provide finance is dragging down the whole economy. Even when they are cleaned up, they will be smaller than they were before. The only way of getting a healthy European financial system that can fund jobs and growth is to build up non-bank finance. That's why Mario Draghi, ECB president, and Mark Carney, governor of the Bank of England, put forward plans in mid-2014 to revive "securitisation" – the business of packaging up loans and turning them into instruments that can be traded on the market. Similar initiatives are needed for other types of non-bank finance. Jean-Claude Juncker, the Commission's president-elect, backed the idea of creating a capital markets union in his inaugural address to the European Parliament. All this is a huge opportunity for the City, as the bulk of this business would be routed through London – provided, of course, Britain stays in the EU.

Chapter Five
Who Wears The Pants?

By joining the EU, the UK surrendered some freedom of action. Eurosceptics don't like that. But, by being part of a larger group of nations, we gained clout. This sort of trade-off is not unique to our membership of the EU. We are, for example, a Nato member. That commits us to go to war to defend the likes of Turkey, Portugal and Estonia. But you don't find lots of eurosceptics arguing that we should pull out of Nato. And quite right too.

In any case, the notion that EU membership has turned us into a vassal of Brussels is nonsense. Our politicians in Westminster decide most things that matter to our people – such as policies for the NHS, education, the economy, law and order, defence and foreign affairs. Only 2% of what our government spends is routed through Brussels; 98% is spent at home without interference by the EU.

The EU affects us not just through money but also laws. But, again, the idea peddled by eurosceptics that we are being dictated to by Brussels is an exaggeration. Only 7% of our primary legislation and 14% of our secondary legislation from 1997-2009 "had a role" in implementing our EU obligations, according to research by the House of Commons

Library[25]. What's more, "the degree of involvement varied from passing reference to explicit implementation". When matters are decided in Brussels, our government has the capacity to veto a lot of things that are of vital national interest. In cases where it doesn't, it still has influence by working with allies both to shape decisions that are in our interest and block decisions that are not. We also have a say on who runs the EU's institutions. So when Brussels "imposes" its will on us, we typically have a hand in the imposing.

Talk to French, Spanish or even German officials and they would say that the British have been astonishingly successful in making the EU in its own image. We won the first battles over whether to turn it into a single market. We also won the battle to enlarge the EU to the east. And English has inexorably become the EU's working language. They even use it in the European Central Bank, despite Britain not being in the single currency.

Europe's nations have agreed a series of treaties about what the EU should do and how it should do it. These have been agreed unanimously. The first was the Treaty of Rome, signed in 1957 by six countries led by France, Germany and Italy. This established a common market and a Common Agricultural Policy (CAP). It also contained the famous phrase calling for "an ever closer union among the peoples of Europe". Often the phrase is truncated to "ever closer union", which can give the impression that Europe is heading towards a super-state. But the full phrase doesn't have that connotation. EU heads of government did clarify this at their summit in June 2014, saying: "The European Council noted that the concept of ever closer union allows for different paths of integration for different countries, allowing those that want to deepen integration to move ahead, while respecting the wish of those who do not want to deepen any further."[12] The language could be sharpened up – say by changing the last clause to "acknowledging that those who do not want to deepen any further are not expected to." Ideally this would be embedded in a new treaty but, otherwise, a new declaration by heads of government would be sufficient.

Britain decided not to sign the Treaty of Rome. When a few years later our government changed its mind, France's President Charles de Gaulle twice blocked our entry. It was only in 1973, after de Gaulle had died, that we finally joined what was then called the European Economic Community (EEC). In the meantime, quite a few of the rules of the game – especially how the CAP operated – had been written in ways that weren't in our interests. Although there's no use crying over spilt milk, note how our interests get damaged when we are not sitting around the table.

The treaties determine the EU's so-called "competences". That's a fancy way of saying what it has the authority to do. It does not mean the EU discharges these functions competently.

After the Treaty of Rome, the other most important treaties have been the Single European Act (1986), which paved the way for launch of the single market, and the Maastricht Treaty (1992), which led to the single currency. We also agreed to other treaties – Amsterdam (1997), Nice (2001), and Lisbon (2007) – which have not been so earth-shattering, but have still transferred further power to Brussels. The treaties have been consolidated into two documents: the Treaty on European Union and the Treaty on the Functioning of the European Union.

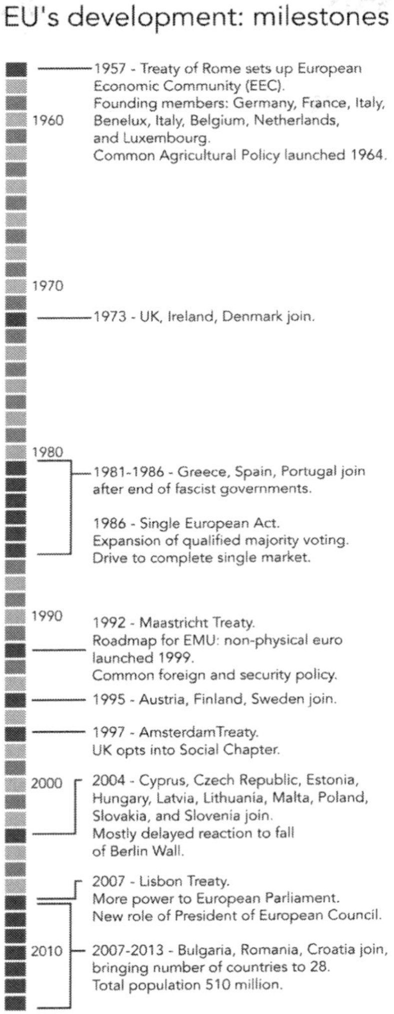

EU's development: milestones
1957 - Treaty of Rome sets up European Economic Community (EEC). Founding members: Germany, France, Italy, Benelux, Italy, Belgium, Netherlands, and Luxembourg. Common Agricultural Policy launched 1964.
1960
1970
1973 - UK, Ireland, Denmark join.
1980
1981-1986 - Greece, Spain, Portugal join after end of fascist governments.
1986 - Single European Act. Expansion of qualified majority voting. Drive to complete single market.
1990
1992 - Maastricht Treaty. Roadmap for EMU: non-physical euro launched 1999. Common foreign and security policy.
1995 - Austria, Finland, Sweden join.
1997 - AmsterdamTreaty. UK opts into Social Chapter.
2000
2004 - Cyprus, Czech Republic, Estonia, Hungary, Latvia, Lithuania, Malta, Poland, Slovakia, and Slovenia join. Mostly delayed reaction to fall of Berlin Wall.
2007 - Lisbon Treaty. More power to European Parliament. New role of President of European Council.
2010
2007-2013 - Bulgaria, Romania, Croatia join, bringing number of countries to 28. Total population 510 million.

In addition to the original competences over the common market, trade and agriculture, the EU's main competences are now home affairs, environment, social policy and regional policy. The EU also has competence over many aspects of macroeconomic policy, though most of this concerns only those countries which are in the euro zone and, hence, not the UK.

The flow of power from Westminster to Brussels is one of the main reasons why people want to quit the EU. A common argument is that Edward Heath, the prime minister who took us into Europe, sold us a pup. In a television broadcast at the time, he said: "There are some in this country who fear that in going into Europe we shall in some way sacrifice independence and sovereignty. These fears, I need hardly say, are completely unjustified."

Heath didn't just make misleading statements. He didn't give the people a referendum on whether to join the then EEC. This was a mistake, although it was partly remedied two years later when Harold Wilson held a plebiscite to ratify our membership after some minor renegotiations.

Whenever power is transferred to the EU, it is hard to get it back. That's why the people should be consulted on new treaties. Unfortunately, we haven't done this. Thatcher didn't call a referendum to ratify the Single European Act, nor did John Major after he signed the Maastricht Treaty, nor did Tony Blair when he decided to opt into the so-called Social Chapter.

Gordon Brown should also have called a referendum on the Lisbon Treaty – not least because Labour had promised a plebiscite on a planned EU constitutional treaty. Although that never materialised because the French and Dutch voted "no" in referendums called to ratify it, most of the ideas were repackaged in the Lisbon Treaty. So Labour effectively broke its promise. In opposition, David Cameron gave a "cast-iron guarantee" that he'd hold a referendum on the Lisbon Treaty if he became prime minister. Two years later, after every other country ratified the treaty, he had to eat his words.

The coalition government has passed legislation saying that there will be a referendum if there is any further transfer of power to the EU. Although this "referendum lock" is the right approach, it is seen by many people as too little, too late. It's partly because of the broken promises by both Labour and the Conservatives that a head of steam has now built up to pull out of the EU entirely.

The fact that the UK should have had referendums to approve the transfer of powers to the EU doesn't mean we should have one in 2017, as Cameron would like, to decide whether to pull out of the EU entirely. If the people were keen on a plebiscite, that would be another matter. They do say they would want a vote when asked. But that desire is not deep. Opinion polls show that the EU is low on the list of the electorate's priorities, even for UKIP voters. Only 8% of the population thought the EU was the most important issue facing the country in May 2014, according to Ipsos Mori. That's down from the 43% who thought it was in 1997 when the debate over whether Britain should join the euro was raging. What's more, there is a risk that Cameron's choice of date won't be the best time to reflect on our EU membership. If he had only the country's interests in mind, he would not have announced in 2013 that there should be a referendum in 2017. The extremely early announcement was an unsuccessful ploy to buy off opposition from eurosceptics in the Conservative Party. Meanwhile, the 2017 date was a stab in the dark – hoping that, by then, there would be another treaty revamping the euro zone and the EU, which would allow the UK to negotiate a new relationship with our partners.

As it is, it currently looks unlikely that there will be anything other than minor treaty changes by 2017. It may take a few more years beyond that before the dust has settled on the euro crisis – and the shape of the EU and our role in it – is clear. As a result, we may end up voting on whether to quit when things are still up in the air. For those who think democracy should be based on informed debate, that would not be good. The Labour and LibDem promise of an IN/OUT referendum when and if there is a further transfer of powers to Brussels is a better plan.

European Council: the top dog

In an ideal world, the EU's governments would get together to decide what they wanted in what is known as the European Council. The European Commission would then get on with the job of implementing what had been decided, in particular completing the single market, and make sure governments follow agreed rules and don't cheat. If there were disputes, the European Court of Justice would then determine who was right and, if necessary, punish the miscreants.

This is a rough description of how the EU works with two important caveats. First, the Commission has a tendency to meddle in things best left to national governments while not doing enough on the really important topic – ensuring fair play in the single market. Second, the European Parliament is also part of the picture and its power has kept growing. It too has an incentive to suck as much power as possible to Brussels and away from nation states, as it did in mid-2014 with the battle over who would run the European Commission.

HOW THE EU WORKS

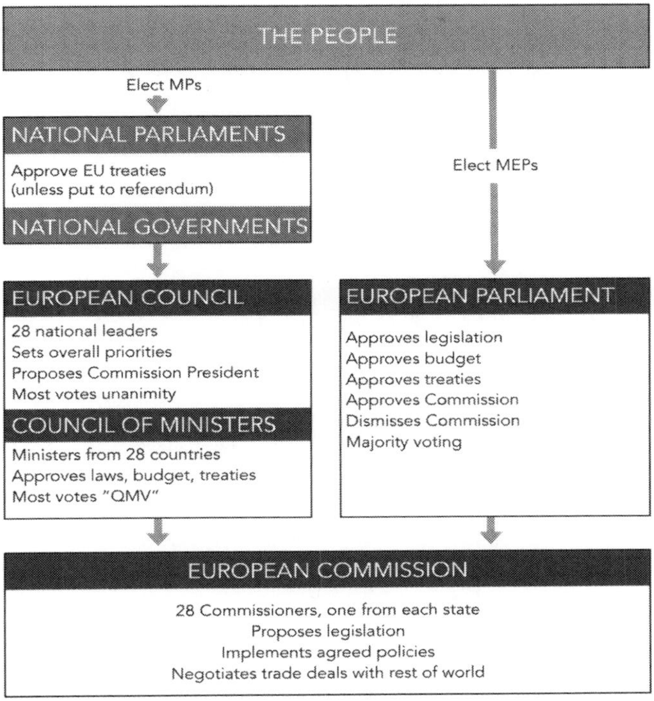

That said, the system works reasonably well. The European Council is the top dog. It is the vehicle through which national governments make their views known. The European Council gathers together the leaders of all 28 countries – people like David Cameron, Germany's Angela Merkel and France's Francois Hollande. It sets the EU's direction and priorities. Closely linked to the European Council is the Council of Ministers, which gathers the relevant government ministers on any topic. The Council has to approve every new directive, the EU's term for a law.[26]

The European Council's power also comes from the fact that it has a big say over who runs the Commission, although it effectively allowed the European Parliament to dictate that Juncker became president in mid-2014. It is important that it does not allow this to become a precedent. Otherwise, power will have shifted from national parliaments to Brussels without the people agreeing to it.

Each country also gets to nominate one of its own citizens as a commissioner. These are typically former politicians such as Peter Mandelson, Leon Brittan and Roy Jenkins. The European Council as a whole engages in horse-trading to decide who get the important jobs – though the European Parliament can veto the entire slate if it doesn't like it.

One of the main eurosceptic gripes is that we can't veto everything we dislike in the Council of Ministers. This is because decisions there are normally taken by what is known as qualified majority voting (QMV). From November 2014, this will mean that, for decisions to pass, at least 55% of the countries have to be in favour and they have to represent at least 65% of the EU's population.

But we (and other governments) do have a veto on several topics, the most important being tax, defence and foreign policy. With social security and criminal justice, there's a further procedure known as an "emergency brake". This allows any country which believes proposed legislation will affect fundamental aspects of its social security or justice system to escalate the matter to the European Council, where unanimity is required. If a deal can't be reached, those countries that want to go ahead can do so on their own.

QMV is the way of dealing with other matters – such as the single market, the environment and social legislation. Given that Britain contains only 12.5% of the EU's population, it doesn't have a veto. To block legislation, it typically needs the support of around a quarter of the other countries – depending on how big they are. Meanwhile, to pass laws, we need to get at least half the other countries onside. This is entirely appropriate. If every country had a veto on everything, nothing would get decided. The EU would rapidly turn into little more than a talking shop like the United Nations.

That is why Margaret Thatcher agreed to the first big use of QMV in the Single European Act, signed in 1986. Here's how she justified it in the House of Lords several years later:

"We would never have got the single market without an extension—not the beginning, but an extension—of majority voting. We could never have got our insurance into Germany—where they promptly kept it out—unless we had majority voting. We could never have got a fair deal for our ships in picking up goods from other ports as others could pick up from ours. We could never have got a fair deal for our lorry and transport business because our lorries had to go over there full and come back empty as they were not allowed to pick up on the way back. Yes, we wanted a single market and we had, in fact, to have some majority voting."

Since 1986, QMV has been extended into areas where it is not necessary, especially social legislation. This became particularly damaging after we opted into the EU's Social Chapter in 1997. We should remedy the error if the treaties are reopened. Probably the most realistic way of achieving this would be to give countries an emergency brake over new social legislation.

European Commission: the eurocracy

When eurosceptics complain about Brussels or "eurocrats", they are normally referring to the Commission. There are three main complaints: that it is wasteful; that it meddles in things it shouldn't; and that it doesn't do enough to enforce the rules.

The first criticism is fair enough. As *The Economist* put it in 2013: "There is plenty of fat to trim: generous tax breaks, far higher average pay than in national governments and benefits that include a 16% expat top-up and payment for children's education until they are 26."

But it's important to get things in proportion. In total, the Commission has 23,000 civil servants. That's fewer than those employed by Birmingham City Council[27]. The cost of running the administration is 6% of the EU's total budget which, in turn, is 1% of EU GDP.

The second criticism about Commission meddling is valid, but it is less of a problem than it was because the eurocrats have recently been driven onto the back foot. The rise in euroscepticism over the past decade and the euro crisis, which the Commission is widely perceived to have managed poorly, are responsible. As a result, the Commission has found it hard to drum up enthusiasm for big new projects, except those relating to the crisis. What's more, even in this area, euro zone governments, especially Germany's, and the European Central Bank have taken most of the key decisions.

The Commission's partial marginalisation contrasts with the vigour of its early days after the Treaty of Rome and of the period 1985-1995 when Jacques Delors was its president. In the first period, there was enthusiasm for building something new; in the second, Delors and his colleagues both pushed through the single market and paved the way for the single currency. The latter initiative – which was dictated more by the political desire to create an ever closer Europe than by economic need – was a classic example of over-reach.

It is good there is less triumphalism in Brussels. But that doesn't mean everything the Commission proposes amounts to meddling. It has played a positive role in advocating open markets, for example driving down mobile phone prices and freeing up air travel. As previously mentioned, we also need a Commission that has the confidence to take initiatives to complete the single market even if that ruffles feathers in national capitals.

This point is acknowledged even by mild eurosceptic MPs such as Andrea Leadsom, who leads the Conservative Fresh Start group. Talking about the need to liberalise trade in services in 2013, she said: "The irony on this occasion is that, whereas most of the time we suffer from too much EU, in this instance we are paying the price for too little EU."

One of the problems is that there are 28 commissioners, one from each country however small it is. They all have an incentive to dream up pet schemes (which adds to the meddling) but there are too many of them to constitute an effective management team. Sometimes, the posts are filled by second-rate has-beens. The ideal solution would be to halve the number – with big countries such as Germany and Britain always having a commissioner and the smaller countries such as Malta and Estonia taking posts by rotation. But it is hard to see this ever being agreed. A good fallback, which might be politically feasible, would be to distinguish between senior commissioners and junior ones. Each senior one would coordinate the work of perhaps three junior ones in the same way that British cabinet ministers have several junior ministers working for them.

The third criticism, that the Commission doesn't police the rules adequately, is partly fair. But the main blame lies with national governments which drag their heels when implementing agreed EU legislation at home. That said, the Commission is cracking the whip. At the end of 2012, it had 1,343 "infringement procedures" open against EU nations. Top of the list of the naughty kids was Italy, which was subject to 99 proceedings. Britain wasn't far behind, with 61 proceedings.

We are better off having the Commission acting as a strong referee than having a free for all. Think of Britain's mad cow crisis in the late 1990s. After the Commission gave our beef the all clear, France continued to block imports. Paris only opened up its market after the European Court of Justice ruled that it was acting illegally and threatened to fine it £100,000 a day.

Similarly, Brussels plays a vital role in competition policy. It stops governments subsidising national companies and tilting the playing field to the disadvantage of rivals from other EU countries. For example, it has cracked down on illegal subsidies by the Italian government to Alitalia, the inefficient bankrupt airline.

The Commission investigates monopolies and cartels, imposing stiff fines if it discovers anti-competitive practices. It can also block cross-border mergers above a certain size if it concludes these are likely to lock up the market to the detriment of consumers. All of this is in our interests.

The Commission is even willing to go head-to-head with big non-EU companies that are distorting the market. For example, it forced Microsoft to unbundle part of its Windows operating system to spur competition, and fined the company 1.4 billion (£1.1 billion). As of early 2014, the Commission was battling Gazprom, the Russian gas giant, for allegedly abusing its dominance in eastern Europe. It is hard to see Britain having the gumption to stand up to a Microsoft or Gazprom all on its own.

European Parliament: democracy without demos

The original European Parliament, or Assembly as it was then called, had little power. It was consulted on legislation but couldn't block it. It also was made up of MPs seconded from national parliaments. It might have been better if it had been kept like that. Indeed, Boris Johnson suggested in 2014 returning to this system with the MPs who were seconded to Brussels being chosen by lottery. It's a nice idea but not practical politics.

Since 1979, members of the European Parliament (MEPs) have been directly elected by the voters. Meanwhile, with successive treaty changes, the Parliament's power has grown. It now has an equal say with the Council on the EU's budget, almost all legislation and foreign treaties.

Eurosceptics love lambasting the Parliament for waste. This is partly because it shuttles back and forth between Brussels and Strasbourg every month. MEPs themselves would like to abolish the Strasbourg parliament – a move that would save £131 million a year and 20,000 tonnes of carbon dioxide emissions. But France is unlikely to agree.

UKIP has also made a lot of noise about how MEPs are well paid and have generous travel and research allowances. This, though, hasn't stopped Farage and his colleagues milking the system to their own advantage. He didn't just employ his wife with taxpayers' money, despite originally promising to do nothing of the sort; he also refused to submit his expenses to an independent audit despite saying he would.

Still, there are bigger worries than waste. One is how the Conservative Party has marginalised itself in the European Parliament. It used to be part of the main centre-right group, the European People's Party (EPP), alongside Angela Merkel's German Christian Democrats and similar parties from France, Spain and so forth.

But Cameron promised to pull out the EPP as a sop to eurosceptics during his campaign to become Tory leader in 2005. So now Conservative MEPs sit with a fringe group called the European Conservatives and Reformists. As a result, their influence – and, hence, Britain's influence, within the Parliament – has declined. This self-inflicted wound has become increasingly damaging as the Parliament's power has risen.

Another worry is the Parliament's desire to accumulate power at the expense of national governments. Consider its behaviour over the Working Time Directive in 2008. The Council and even the Commission wanted to amend the legislation to make clear that when doctors are on-call but asleep at their workplace, those hours don't count towards the maximum 48 hours a week they are allowed to work. The Parliament said it wasn't prepared to amend the directive unless all the countries which had secured partial opt-outs from the legislation, including Britain, surrendered them.

The biggest worry stems from the Parliament's increasing say over who runs the Commission. Not only can it reject whomever is proposed by the European Council; the European Council is supposed to propose a Commission President after taking account of the European elections. The Parliament can also reject the entire Commission when it's appointed if it doesn't like it – and it can dismiss it at any time with a two-thirds majority.

The Parliament is trying to use these powers to turn the Commission into a government answerable to it rather than to nation states. The main ideological blocs each picked a candidate to represent them in the 2014 European Parliament elections. They declared that whichever bloc got the most number of MEPs would have the right to install its candidate as the Commission's President.

This was a naked power grab by the Parliament, to which national leaders should never have agreed. But they didn't appreciate the importance of the constitutional change when the candidates were chosen in 2013 and early 2014. In the end, the EPP came first and its MEPs (along with those from other groups) demanded that its standard-bearer, Jean-Claude Juncker, be appointed Commission President. Cameron tried to fight a last-ditch battle against this. But he mishandled the diplomacy and Juncker was nominated anyway. The folly of pulling the Conservatives out of the EPP then became glaringly apparent.

This would not matter so much if the European electorate really felt European – or, as political scientists put it, if there was a European "demos". But, according to the Commission's spring 2013 Eurobarometer survey, only 22% of respondents feel they are "definitely" EU citizens with another 40% feeling they are EU citizens "to some extent". The fact that we don't have a single European demos is also manifested by the low turnout of European elections. In 2014, 43% of the EU electorate voted, down from 62% in 1979. In the UK, the number was just 34%. The turnout in UK general elections has also been dropping but it was still 65% in 2010.

What's more, when people vote in European elections they often don't vote on European issues. Many treat it as an opportunity to cast a protest vote against the incumbent government at home, just as they do in local elections. That's one reason UKIP came first in 2014. Voters who wanted to protest against the coalition didn't have the normal option of voting Liberal Democrat because it is part of the coalition. Nick Clegg, the LibDem leader, also performed badly in his debates with Farage. Meanwhile, those on the centre-right didn't want to vote Labour. UKIP became the protest part of default. There is a danger that the European Parliament's growing power will lead to pseudo-democracy rather than real democracy.. Cameron did persuade other leaders to review the process of appointing the Commission President at the June 2014 summit. He now needs to get a strong declaration to the effect that the manner of Juncker's nomination does not constitute a precedent and work out an acceptable alternative procedure. We should also seek to build up the power of national parliaments as a counterweight.

European Court of Human Rights

The European institution that really gets up eurosceptics' noses is the European Court of Human Rights (ECHR). It has recently caused controversy by making it difficult for the UK to send Abu Qatada, the firebrand Muslim cleric, to Jordan for trial. It has also ruled that we cannot have a blanket ban on prisoners voting.

One will often hear people rail against the ECHR and give its behaviour as a reason for quitting the EU. But whatever we think about the ECHR, we should realise that – unlike the European Court of Justice which is the EU's supreme court and can, among other things, punish governments for cheating – the ECHR isn't an EU institution. It was set up by a totally different treaty, the European Convention on Human Rights. Any new country joining the

EU has to sign the Convention. But Britain is not in that position. So we might be able retract our signature to the Convention without quitting the EU.

Whether that would be wise is another matter. Although the ECHR made it tough for us to get rid of Abu Qatada, we were finally able to do so in 2013. We just had to go through extra hoops to reduce the risk that the Jordanian government would use evidence gained through torture when it tried him. Was that such a bad thing? However much we dislike somebody, would we really want evidence extracted by torture being used to convict him? And even though it may be irritating to be told we can't ban every prisoner from voting, we are still able to stop the worst criminals from doing so.

More generally, it would send a bad message to the rest of the world if Britain pulled out of the Convention. We would lose some of our moral authority to tell tyrants in, say, Syria and Zimbabwe that they should stop abusing human rights. The easy riposte would be: "Who are you to lecture us about human rights? You've retracted your signature to the European Convention on Human Rights".

An alternative idea, which the Conservative Party may adopt as a manifesto commitment for the 2015 general election, is to give MPs the right to veto any ECHR rulings they don't like. Dominic Grieve, who was sacked as attorney-general in July 2014 apparently because he disagreed with this move, told *The Times* it would drive "a coach and horses through international legal obligations, behaving in a way that can only be described as anarchic." Parliamentary sovereignty was "open to misuse", he said. "You could enact through parliament to have someone summarily executed. You could require the whole United Kingdom to worship the moon, but we don't do this and we don't do it because it would be wrong. In exactly the same way it would be thoroughly wrong for parliament to use its power to defy an international treaty obligation." In his devastating interview, the former attorney-general added: "It's not dissimilar from Putin using the Duma to ratify his annexation of the Crimea. Putin will say, well it's now lawful; the Duma has said so."

Democratic deficit

It is often argued that the EU is inadequately democratic or that it has a "democratic deficit". This is exaggerated. After all, the European Council is still the EU's most powerful body and it is made up of national leaders, all of whom are democratically elected. Some national parliaments also do a good job in holding their leaders to account. German, Danish and Swedish MPs, for example, insist on their ministers getting approval for their negotiating strategies before they go to the European Council/Council of Ministers. Our parliament doesn't do this. But it could and should quiz the prime minister and ministers before they head off to Brussels to negotiate on our behalf, something Labour is advocating. It is also proposing that MPs can veto the PM's nominee for Britain's EU commissioner. This is a good idea. It is more democratic and less likely to result in low-profile politicians – such as Jonathan Hill, the new commissioner, or Cathy Ashton, his predecessor – being appointed to the job.

The power of national parliaments was boosted by two new tools in the Lisbon Treaty: a yellow card and an orange card. These are supposed to shore up "subsidiarity", the principle under which the EU is only supposed to take action if it can do so more effectively than a nation state can alone. The yellow card specifies that, if a third of national parliaments consider that the Commission has breached the subsidiarity principle, it has to think again. The orange card says that, if half national parliaments take this view, the Commission has to backtrack or justify its position in front of both the Council and the European Parliament.

The yellow and orange cards are useful innovations. The yellow card was used first in 2012 in connection with a proposed EU law clarifying the right to strike. Twelve parliaments, including the UK's, protested – after which the Commission backed down.

The card was used again in 2013 when parliaments in 11 countries including Britain objected to the Commission's plans to create an EU prosecution office. Unfortunately, the Commission dug its heels in, arguing the proposal complied with the principle of subsidiarity. This shows the weaknesses of the current system. The cards can't block new laws. What's more, they can only be used if subsidiarity has been contravened and, even then, only with new legislation.

More could and should be done to increase the power of national governments. One idea is to upgrade the orange card to a red one. So, if half national parliaments objected to a proposed law, the Commission would have to drop it. Both the yellow card and this new red card could be further strengthened by allowing national parliaments to object for any reason – not just on grounds of subsidiarity.

But the problem isn't just with new laws. National parliaments also need a way to repeal or amend the pile of existing EU laws that are clogging up the statute books. A new green card could be used to do this. Under this, the Commission would have to come up with a new proposal if half national parliaments wanted an existing law repealed or amended. A good candidate for amendment would be the Working Time Directive. It would still have to go through the European Parliament, which might veto the change. But if enough national parliaments objected, their greater legitimacy might force the issue.

Introducing new green and red cards would require treaty changes, in the same way that getting an emergency brake for social legislation would. If the treaties are reopened, these reforms should be on our wish list. If not, as a fallback option, we should push for the Commission to agree that it will in future treat orange cards as if they were red.

Chapter Six
EU's Crown Jewel: The Single Market

Access to the single market is the most important reason for Britain to stay in the EU. But what exactly is the single market and how beneficial is it for us?

The EU's free market has gone through various versions. Version 1.0 was what used to be called the common market, established by the Treaty of Rome. It was underpinned by the "four freedoms": the free movement of goods, services, labour and people. The idea was that there would be free trade throughout what was then called the European Economic Community (EEC). Tariff barriers, or import taxes, were abolished between the original six members by 1968.

The countries also agreed to have a common external tariff. So France, Germany, Italy and the others imposed the same taxes on imports from outside the EEC. That was necessary. Otherwise, goods from, say, Japan could have come into the EEC via the country with the lowest tariffs and then circulated freely through the rest of the common market without paying any extra tax. The combination of free trade within the EEC and a common external tariff is known as a customs union. This was the system Britain joined in 1973.

Single market milestones

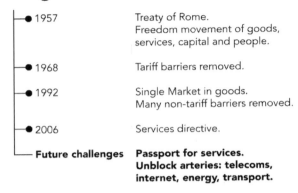

1957	Treaty of Rome. Freedom movement of goods, services, capital and people.
1968	Tariff barriers removed.
1992	Single Market in goods. Many non-tariff barriers removed.
2006	Services directive.
Future challenges	**Passport for services. Unblock arteries: telecoms, internet, energy, transport.**

Free markets and trade bring big economic benefits. If people are free to buy goods and services from abroad, they can shop around for the best prices and quality. It's not just ordinary consumers that benefit. Companies are consumers too. If they get a better deal on what they buy from other companies, they will make more profits and give their own customers a better deal. The same logic works for governments, the biggest consumers of all. If they can shop around, they should be able to offer better quality public services and/or need to tax their people less than they otherwise would. Meanwhile, if companies are free to sell abroad, they can expand, create good jobs and generate wealth.

Similar arguments apply to the free movement of people and capital. Workers have more opportunities for interesting and well-remunerated careers if they are free to work anywhere within the EU. Companies have a larger pool of employees to choose from – allowing them to attract higher skilled or cheaper labour. Equally, when capital is free to move around, investors can get better returns on their money and successful firms can raise capital more easily and so grow faster.

Free trade also allows countries to specialise in what they do best. Take pharmaceuticals. The UK has expertise in making drugs, based on a strong research base and a 200-year track record. Two of the world's pharma giants – GlaxoSmithKline and AstraZeneca – are headquartered here. A number of other EU countries, especially France and Germany, are also fairly strong in drugs. But most are not. It can take 15 years to develop, test and get regulatory approval for a new drug. Scientists need to investigate thousands of chemicals before hitting on a successful compound. Rather than every country trying to invent and then manufacture cutting-edge pharmaceuticals, an efficient market drives expertise into concentrated hubs.

This specialisation and concentration leads to economies of scale. If a company can operate on a larger scale, it can get more efficient. The money it invests in research, manufacturing, marketing and so forth can be recouped by selling to the whole EU, and indeed global, market rather than having to be charged to just one national market. As it ramps up production, its average costs go down. EU consumers benefit, provided lower costs are passed through in the form of lower prices.

Economies of scale occur in a wide range of industries where Britain has an edge – not just pharmaceuticals, but cars, the City, creative industries and legal services.

Jet engines are a good example. New technology has to be developed and thoroughly tested to make sure it is safe. Britain's Rolls-Royce spends over £900 million a year on research and development. If each EU country built its own engines, their cost would be so prohibitive that none would be competitive. As it is, Rolls is the only European company at the top end of the market competing against America's General Electric and Pratt & Witney. Economies of scale allow it to invest in new technology and win customers on a global scale.

To ensure that economies of scale and efficiencies actually benefit consumers, there has to be competition between suppliers. If a single company can get a lock on a market or, by working with rivals, form a cartel, consumers will not benefit. Equally, if governments are allowed to subsidise national champions, that will prevent free and fair trade. The subsidised company will win more market share than it deserves, knocking out more efficient firms.

This is why competition policy has always been an essential part of the common market. The Commission has the power to investigate and punish monopolies and cartels, stop governments subsidising companies and block mergers that would be anti-competitive. Over the years, it has got better at promoting competition. Particular progress was made when Britain's Leon Brittan was competition commissioner from 1989 to 1993.

Vigorous competition between firms has another advantage. When companies face the heat from rivals, they are spurred on to become more efficient and innovate. Being part of a large single market, therefore, has many benefits for the UK. What's more, over the years, that market has got bigger and bigger. When we joined the then EEC, it had 257 million consumers. Now it has 510 million. In 2012, its GDP was $16.1 trillion. That's a little bigger than America, whose large internal market is one of the sources of its economic success. Its GDP was $15.7 trillion.

This is not to suggest, for one moment, that the EU should create a "fortress Europe", having a strong internal market but erecting barriers to trade with the rest of the world. For the same reasons that Britain benefits from the EU's single market, it benefits from free trade across the globe. We, therefore, need to do everything we can to pry open markets elsewhere.

1992 and all that

The common market was a big leap forward for trade within Europe. But it did not deliver the Treaty of Rome's goal of full barrier-free trade. The main reason is the difference between what are called tariff barriers and non-tariff barriers. Non-tariff barriers are rules, regulations and other practices that make it difficult for goods and services to be sold across national frontiers. Examples include rules that cars must have brakes that conform to a specific national standard; that ski instructors must have passed a local exam; that companies wishing to supply the government must be based in its country; or that food must adhere to national hygiene standards.

Many of these practices are justified on the grounds that they are needed to protect health, safety, consumers or the environment. But they are often used to shut out competition. Vested interests benefit; consumers suffer.

Such non-tariff barriers are less visible and more insidious than tariff barriers. So even when tariffs were abolished within the then EEC, a lot of trade got gummed up. There was, therefore, a new drive from the mid-1980s to complete the common market, which was then rechristened the single market. The plan was to sweep away non-tariff barriers. The initiative was spearheaded by Arthur Cockfield, a British commissioner, and strongly backed by Margaret Thatcher. A deadline of end 1992 was set.

How, though, do you sweep away a non-tariff barrier? The answer is that you have to pass regulations. This is one of the ironies of creating the internal market: in order to get rid of national rules that restrict trade, you have to pass new EU ones that open it up.

A good example is the humble lawnmower. In the early 1990s, when John Major was prime minister, the EU imposed an upper limit on their decibel level. Eurosceptics saw it as an example of Brussels over-reaching itself. This is how Philip Stephens, a *Financial Times* columnist, tells the story[28]:

"Caught off-guard, ministers demanded an investigation. How had it got through? Why had Britain failed to kick up a fuss? Back came Whitehall officials with the story. Yes, there was indeed such a directive, they reported. No, Her Majesty's Government had not opposed it. Worse, it had voted in favour of the regulation. Even worse, Britain had proposed the directive and subsequently steered its passage through the Council of Ministers!

"There was a simple explanation. The Germans, it seemed, had set a national noise limit on lawnmowers to ensure the peace and quiet of that country's good burghers during the summer cutting season. The problem – and was it coincidental? – was that this excluded imports of the noisier products of British-owned manufacturers. A level playing field within the single market demanded EU regulation that stopped Germany from unfairly locking out the competition. Sure enough, the new, Europe-wide, decibel ceiling put the British producers back in the game."

Look too at what local and national governments around the EU spend on goods and services. Such "public procurement" is 19% of EU GDP. Most governments would have a bias for awarding contracts to local firms if there wasn't a rule telling them that they are not allowed to discriminate against companies from other EU nations. This rule is needed not just to give all firms a fair chance to win contracts; it means that governments (and, hence, taxpayers) get a better deal.

You also often need rules to set minimum standards to protect consumers, the environment, health and safety. You can call these rules red tape if you like. But, without some regulations, many markets would stay shut and those that were opened would be subject to a free-for-all which could harm consumers.

Eurosceptics often complain that all our companies have to follow EU rules, even those that don't export to the EU. But businesses like the fact that there are common product standards across the EU because they don't have to follow different specifications for different markets. When the Confederation of British Industry surveyed its members in 2013, 52% said common product standards were positive for their business; only 15% said they were negative. If we quit the EU and decided to develop our own product rules, our exporters would be at a disadvantage. They'd have to follow one set of rules at home and another if they wanted to sell to the EU. Then they'd really be fuming about red tape.

Complaints about British industry being strangled by red tape are exaggerated. The UK's product market regulations are less restrictive than those of other EU countries, according to the OECD. They are even less restrictive than those of other Anglo-Saxon countries such as America, Canada, Australia and New Zealand. What's more, product regulations got easier in the decade from to 2008, the last date the OECD has assessed.

Meanwhile, our labour markets are more liberal than those of other EU countries and on a par with other Anglo-Saxon countries. Despite being in the EU, we haven't had to follow many continental European practices for protecting permanent workers from dismissal.

The UK ranked 10th out of 148 countries in the World Economic Forum's 2013/14 Global Competitiveness Index.

Four other EU countries – Germany, Finland, Sweden and the Netherlands – were in the top 10 too. So being in the EU does not automatically tie a country's industry in knots.

What's more, not all the red tape can be blamed on Brussels. For a start, the UK has occasionally "gold-plated" EU legislation. This means we sometimes take an EU law and embellish it when we turn it into a British one. This is a problem entirely of our own making. See below for how we've done this with the Working Time Directive. The coalition government has, thankfully, promised not to gold-plate EU laws in the future and to remove unnecessary gold-plate from existing laws. But this promise needs to be toughened up. Why not pass a law saying all gold-plate has to be removed by a deadline of say 2020 unless the government can justify why it is needed?

War on red tape

None of this is to suggest that all the rules adopted to promote the single market are necessary or good. Sometimes the EU has taken a heavy-handed approach of harmonising standards. The biggest problems are in social, environmental and health and safety legislation.

The Commission still comes up with silly ideas like its plan in mid-2013 to ban olive oil jugs in restaurants on "health" grounds and instead require them to provide oil in individually sealed containers. But this scheme, which seemed to be driven by a desire to promote the interests of olive oil producers rather than consumers, was fortunately withdrawn after a public outcry.

But momentum is building up to cut red tape – with Britain and other countries arguing that doing so is necessary to boost growth. Even the Commission is getting the message. In 2013, it launched a plan nicknamed Refit which is supposed to simplify EU rules. One example it gave was how it had scrapped the notorious ban on "curvy cucumbers". Another was how it had abandoned a "health and safety" measure to stop hairdressers wearing high-heel shoes.

José Manuel Barroso, the Commission President, has also changed his rhetoric in line with the new zeitgeist, saying: "I strongly believe the EU should not meddle in everything that happens in Europe."

One of the most important changes has been the establishment of the EU's Impact Assessment Board in 2006. This Board has the mandate to improve the quality of the Commission's "cost/benefit" analyses for proposed legislation. It doesn't give a view on the merits of the new regulations themselves, but rather on whether the Commission has done a good job in assessing the impact of its proposals.

The Board has sent lots of sub-standard impact assessments back to the Commission and asked it to do more work on them. For example, it concluded that the initial cost-benefit analysis of plans for a free trade deal with United States needed further work. But it doesn't have the ability to block a proposal if the analysis is not up to snuff. One way to improve the system would be to give it this power.

What's more, it isn't just the Commission that should be doing impact assessments. Our own government does them on EU legislation but often doesn't get them to the European Parliament in time to affect the debate. It needs to pull its finger out. Meanwhile, the Council of Ministers hardly ever does cost-benefit analyses of the changes it makes to EU legislation. This isn't good enough.

An assessment of the burden from the EU's top 100 regulations by Open Europe concluded in 2013 that they "cost" the UK economy £27.4 billion a year[29]. It got this figure by totting up all the costs in "cost/benefit analyses" of EU rules conducted by our government.

It is important to realise that this £27.4 billion figure is only the "cost" part of the cost/benefit analysis. Regulations have benefits too. If you tell a company not to pollute the air, that's a cost to it; but cleaner air means people are less likely to get asthma. If you tell banks to hold more capital, that's a cost to them; but it means the financial system is less likely to blow up. And so on. The government's same cost-benefit analyses concluded that the top 100 rules had a combined benefit of £57.1 billion.

These figures suggest that the net benefit to Britain from all this regulation is nearly £30 billion a year. But this should be taken with a pinch of salt for several reasons. First, some of the benefits may be over-estimated. For example, the government thought the EU's climate and energy package would have a benefit of £20.4 billion a year but this was based on the assumption that there would be a global deal to curb climate change, which hasn't materialised. On the other hand, some of the cost-benefit analyses don't quantify the benefits – so some of the positives are under-estimated.

Overall, it seems clear that the benefits exceed the costs. But that doesn't mean we should be happy. After all, the average obscures many sins. In a quarter of cases, the estimated costs exceeded the benefits. One example is the Temporary Agency Workers Directive, which guarantees those who work via employment agencies the same pay and conditions as people who work as employees.

The estimated costs of £2.1 billion were more than the £1.5 billion of benefits. Another example is the Energy Performance of Buildings Directive, where costs of £1.5 billion exceeded benefits of £364 million.

But we shouldn't assume we could cut that much of the red tape if we left the EU. We would certainly be able to amend some of the rules if we didn't have to negotiate everything via Brussels. But it is unrealistic to suppose that we could consign most of them to the bonfire. We'd still need rules to prevent banks blowing up, measures to stop companies discriminating against workers on the basis of sex, age and race, food safety standards and so on.

Does sleep count as work?

If you ask eurosceptics which single EU regulation they hate most, many will point to the Working Time Directive. This says that people are not allowed to work more than 48 hours a week. It also says that employees must receive a minimum four weeks paid holiday, a day off every week, a break every six hours and night shifts that don't last longer than eight hours[30].

The directive is so unpopular, in part, because of the way it was imposed upon us in 1993. At the time Britain was not covered by social rules because our prime minister, John Major, had opted out of the so-called Social Chapter. But the Commission pushed through the legislation on the grounds that it was a health and safety issue. Although the government took the Commission to the European Court of Justice arguing it was overstepping its authority, it lost.

That said, the legislation isn't quite as bad as it looks. This is partly because some of the provisions – such as a break every six hours or a day off every week – are reasonable. If people work without breaks, their health and productivity suffer. Sometimes that can put other people at risk.

The law is also not too damaging because countries are allowed to opt out of key parts of the directive. Britain – along with 15 other countries including Germany – have taken advantage of some or all of these opt-outs. The key one is the cap on working 48 hours a week: with the opt-out, anybody is free to work longer, but nobody can be forced to do so.

But there are still problems with the directive because of the bizarre way the European Court of Justice has interpreted it. In one case, it decided that the time people spend "on call" at their workplace counts towards their working time, even if they are asleep. In another case, it said that workers are entitled to a rest immediately after a working day or night – making 24-hour shifts illegal. In yet another, it said employees can accrue holiday when they are on maternity or long-term sick leave.

These rulings have been costly for the NHS where junior doctors used to work long shifts, often sleeping at hospital for several nights in a row. Even so, the old days of 100-hour weeks weren't that great for either the trainee doctors or their patients.

Both EU governments and the Commission wanted to amend the directive in 2008 to resolve some of these problems, particularly the definition of "on call" time. But the European Parliament refused to back the amended legislation unless all the countries abandoned their opt-outs. That unacceptable demand has led to a stalemate.

A particularly costly part of the directive, though, is something we've brought upon ourselves. In interpreting the requirement that everybody should have four weeks' holiday, our government – under pressure from trade unions – agreed to add the eight annual Bank Holidays on top. So British workers actually get 5.6 weeks paid holiday. This gold-plating costs industry about £3 billion a year. We could avoid this cost by simply changing our own laws in Westminster. There's no need to quit the EU. Given that it would be such a political hot potato to take away people's holidays, it's unlikely that we'd cut the cost of the directive even if we left the EU.

The Working Time Directive is also a great example of how Britain plays by the rules even when it doesn't like them. In 2010, 22 EU states breached at least one of the directive's provisions, according to a report by the Centre for European Reform. But the Commission hadn't taken a single one of them to court. Britain was one of the few states with a clean record. Some say that we, too, should break the law. A better solution might be to take the Commission to court for not upholding the law. That would put a cat among the pigeons and might provide the impetus to reform some of the law's absurdities.

Planes, (not trains) and mobiles

One of the single market's most visible successes has been in air travel. In the old days, individual countries protected their national flag-carriers most of which were state-owned. We had British Airways, the French had Air France, the Germans Lufthansa and so forth. In many cases, only flag-carriers were allowed to take passengers from one country to another – for example, only BA and Air France could fly people from London to Paris – although there was an exception for charter flights. Normally only the national flag-carriers could transport people within a particular country. When the flag-carriers got into financial trouble, taxpayers often bailed them out. The system was rotten: prices were high and the choice of flights was limited.

All this has now changed. In 1992, the market was forced open so that now any EU airline can fly people anywhere within the EU. New airlines, such as Easyjet and Ryanair, have sprung into existence offering cheap, no-frills flights and opening up new routes. The old flag-carriers have had to cut costs to meet the threat. Most have been privatised and the Commission has curtailed the old practice of doling out subsidies to basket cases. Some have cut back their operations; others, such as BA which has merged with Spain's Iberia, have restructured on transnational lines. Between 1992 and 2010, passenger traffic within the EU doubled and the number of intra-EU routes increased by 140%. It is now much easier for Britons to travel around Europe for business or pleasure.

Telecommunications is another, partial, EU success story. The industry used to be a bit like the bad old airline industry. Each country had a national operator, which normally was state-owned and had a monopoly at home. International calls were run by the two monopolists at each end of the line and were exorbitantly expensive. This comfy cartel didn't just keep prices high; the firms were overstaffed and inefficient, while the range of services offered to customers was limited.

Much of this has changed. The UK, under Thatcher, led the way by privatising BT and opening its market to competition in the 1980s. A key new entrant was Vodafone, which got one of Britain's first licences to offer mobile communications. Other countries followed suit. The Commission got into the act, pushing for markets to be opened up to competition.

Brussels has also become increasingly active in driving down "roaming charges". These are the prices people pay for making phone calls when they are outside their home country. They are the mobile equivalent of the old international telecoms cartel. They used to be exorbitant. There were also hefty charges for receiving calls when people roamed. After the latest cuts in July 2014, the cost of using mobiles in other EU countries is getting reasonable, and from the end of 2015 roaming charges will be scrapped entirely.

In the 1980s, the Commission also helped create a European standard for mobile communications known as GSM. Before that, there had been a host of different standards. The single standard allowed Europe's manufacturers – mainly Sweden's Ericsson and Finland's Nokia – to build up economies of scale that then helped them become big global players. The single standard also made it easier for service providers to operate across frontiers. One of the biggest winners was Vodafone which, through a series of acquisitions, built a network across much of the EU and then branched out across the globe. In its evidence to the government's review of EU powers in 2013, it said: "Europe has given British companies like Vodafone the opportunity to acquire scale on the European continent and to use this as a stepping stone into the US, Japan, China and India."

Passport for services

1992 came and went – and a lot was done to remove non-tariff barriers. But a lot was also not done. The main progress was in goods, where there is now pretty much barrier-free trade within the EU. But goods account for only 27% of the EU economy. Services, which account for 73% of the economy, are responsible for just under a quarter of intra-EU trade. For Britain, where services account for 78% of the economy, it is particularly disappointing that these markets are not more open.

The EU did have a crack at liberalising the market when it passed the Services Directive in 2006. But the legislation, advocated by the Commission, was diluted after opposition from various countries – especially France. This tale shows that the Commission is often one of the good guys, rather than the bad guy. It has normally fought for extending free trade within the EU.

The original idea was that services companies should have something akin to a passport. This would mean they would be free to provide services anywhere in the EU so long as they were properly authorised at home. That would be similar to what happens in financial services, where companies based and regulated in the UK can operate anywhere in the EU.

The simplicity of a services passport proved too radical for some of our EU partners. They argued that national rules were still needed to protect consumers from poor-quality services from abroad. They also said professional qualifications were often required to ensure quality. The final compromise required countries to let service providers from other EU countries have access to their markets but allowed them to impose a range of conditions which means companies don't have anything like a passport.

Many countries also still demand that people pass local professional qualifications before they can offer a service. There are an astonishing 800 or so regulated professions in the EU. Of these, only seven – architects, dentists, doctors, midwives, nurses, pharmacist and vets – are automatically recognised in other EU countries[31].

Yet another problem concerns implementation. Even when the EU has agreed to open up a market, there is no guarantee that the market won't stay shut if national governments drag their feet in passing the necessary legislation back home.

To be fair, the Commission has been pressing governments harder to implement the rules – including bringing infringement actions at the European Court of Justice against those that dig their heels in. The Commission says that proper enforcement would boost EU GDP by 1% over the next 5-10 years[32]. This, again, goes to show that Britain needs a Commission that is strong enough to police the single market's rules.

The current Commission has launched a new batch of reforms under the rubric of the Single Market Acts l and ll. This includes useful initiatives such as an EU patent, which should make it cheaper for companies to protect their inventions, and proposals to make it easier for professionals to get their qualifications recognised across borders.

But the bottom line is that services markets are still partially closed – and this is holding the EU economy back. One indication of inefficiency is that the EU has five times as many services companies as the US, an economy roughly the same size.[33] Fragmentation means European companies do not enjoy the economies of scale that their American rivals do – and so are not in a good position to win the battle for global market share.

Prying open services markets would be a big prize for Britain. We are not a lone voice. In 2012, 11 other national leaders including those from Spain, Italy and Poland joined David Cameron in arguing for another drive to complete the single market. The priority should be to get services companies a passport, allowing firms that are properly authorised at home to offer their services anywhere in the EU[34]. The opportunity to do so is a further reason to stay in the EU because we certainly won't be able to achieve this objective if we quit.

Get networking

Another priority should be to open up those network industries that are not covered by the services directive: transport, energy and telecoms. These networks are the economy's arteries. Given that they are blocked up, it is not surprising the EU is not functioning well.

Look at transport. Air travel now works a lot better after the old cartel was broken up. But a patchwork of national air traffic control systems still prevents the EU enjoying a fully open sky. The Commission puts the cost at 5 billion (£4.2 billion) a year. Meanwhile, railways are still largely operating as they did in the bad old days. Although some countries, such as Britain and Germany, allow foreign train companies to operate on their tracks, most do not. Such protectionism denies our rail companies the advantage of operating in a single market – and denies foreign passengers the possibility of cheaper and/or better train travel.

It's a similar story in energy. Britain has opened up its gas and electricity markets to competition by splitting the companies that own the pipelines and the national grid from businesses that supply consumers. Many other EU countries initially resisted attempts by the Commission to force them to do the same. Even after it managed to push that through, the cross-border market in energy hasn't operated effectively because there is not enough infrastructure connecting national gas pipelines and electricity grids with one another.

Finally, the EU is not making the most of the internet and telecoms despite their critical importance to the modern economy. Too many barriers block the free flow of online services and entertainment across national borders. These include a complex web of differing national copyright regimes and the absence of a secure and affordable system for cross-border on-line payments. As a result, only 12% of EU citizens buy online from suppliers in other EU states, according to the European Commission's Eurobarometer survey.

Meanwhile, the telecoms industry's fragmentation puts Europe at a disadvantage to America, where investment in advanced networks is running at higher levels.

Unblocking these arteries should be one of our top goals.

So what's it worth?

Quantifying the benefits to us of the single market is tricky. How do we know, for example, what would have happened if we hadn't been in the EU? There have, however, been multiple academic studies which try to put a value on the single market. Although a few eurosceptic analyses argue that it is damaging for Britain, most studies conclude it has been positive[35]. One 2008 study[36] that looked at the whole period since the creation of the original common market concluded that EU GDP was 5% higher than it would otherwise have been. Meanwhile, the Confederation of British Industry has concluded the benefits of the single market are roughly 4-5% of GDP[37]. A similar conclusion was reached by academics at the LSE. Taking account of trade losses and lower productivity growth, they estimated that Britain would lose between 2.2% and 9.5% of GDP if we quit the EU[38]. The wide variation is explained by the fact that the damage depends very much on what sort of access to the single market we manage to retain.

But this 4-5% figure underestimates the value to us of the single market because it doesn't take account of the benefits we've gained since the admittedly half-hearted liberalisation of services since 2006. Nor does it take account of the possibility that we could get further benefits if we could fully open up the services market, which the UK government thinks would boost UK income per head by 7.1%[39]. As mentioned, the Commission thinks proper implementation of the existing rules are worth an extra 1% to GDP on top of that. The so far unachieved benefits of the single market could therefore be about 8% of GDP.

Now there's precious little chance of opening the services market and implementing the rules fully. But if we could get half the way there – delivering an extra 4% of GDP – the benefit of the single market would be around 9% of GDP. That's an average of £2,200 for every man, woman and child in the country. We shouldn't throw that away lightly.

Chapter Seven
Good, Bad And Ugly

The single market is the EU's crown jewel. But what about all the other kit and caboodle that comes with membership? What are the good, bad and ugly features?

Budget blues

One complaint about the EU is its budget. Eurosceptics think it spends too much money. There is some truth in this criticism, but it is overdone. The EU's budget for the next seven years (2014-2020) is 960 billion (£807 billion). While that's a lot of money in absolute terms, it amounts to 1% of the EU's GDP. To put that in context, the UK's own national budget is 46% of GDP.

Still, 1% of GDP is 1% of GDP. And we should never waste money – especially at a time when we have such a large budget deficit at home. It was, therefore, important that David Cameron along with allies such as Germany's Angela Merkel managed in early 2013 to secure an agreement to cut the EU budget for the next seven years by 3.4% in real terms compared to the previous seven years. A smaller budget will force the EU to focus on priorities and cut waste. Cameron's success is another example of how Britain can often achieve its objectives if it builds alliances.

But will even this reduced budget be well spent? The frank answer is "no". The biggest slice, 39%, will be spent on agriculture and rural communities – policies which fall into the "ugly" camp. Another 34% will be spent on regional policies, which fall into the "bad" camp. These two big policies account for 73% of the EU's spending. Still, even this is an improvement on the previous seven-year period, when they accounted for 77% of spending. So Cameron's budget deal didn't just cut overall spending; it whittled down the proportion of bad spending.

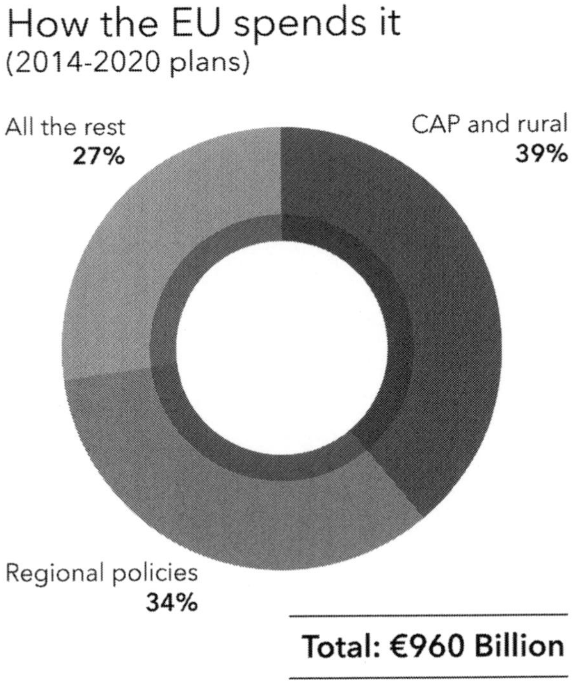

Everything else is chicken-feed by comparison – some of it good (such as research grants), some of it bad (such as the expense of shifting the European Parliament backward and forwards between Strasbourg and Brussels). Again, that doesn't mean we shouldn't improve how the rest of the money is spent – for example, by bearing down on the cost of bureaucracy. But let's get things in proportion. The EU spends 6% of its budget on administration. Reforming the CAP and regional policy further are the priorities.

What about the UK's contribution? This has been a running sore virtually from the moment that we joined the EEC in 1973 and we discovered that we were paying Brussels more money than we were receiving back – despite the fact that we were then one of the poorer nations. The main reason for this was the Common Agricultural Policy. We didn't receive nearly as much money from this slush fund as, say, France because agriculture is a less important part of our economy. Because of various quirks of history, we also get less money per acre than most other countries.

Margaret Thatcher fought a bitter and ultimately successful battle to even things out when she was prime minister. She secured a rebate on part of our contribution to the budget in 1984. Tony Blair gave away some of this rebate in 2005 in the hope that this would lead to further reform of the CAP. It didn't. But we still hung onto most of our rebate.

This is what the numbers look like for the financial year 2013/14[40]. Britain plans to make a "gross contribution" of £17.1 billion. After a rebate of £3.6 billion, our contribution is expected to come down to £13.5 billion. Of this, £5.2 billion is to be recycled back to the UK via the government. The money doesn't stay with the government but, instead, goes mostly to our farmers and to development projects in poor regions such as Cornwall and west Wales. If you subtract this money, our "net" contribution will be £8.3 billion. Again it is worth putting this in context. That's around half a percent of our GDP and just over 1% of our own £720 billion of public spending – or £130 per person.

UK'S EU BUDGET CONTRIBUTION

	£ billion
Gross contribution	17.1
(less rebate)	-3.6
	13.5
(less money recycled to UK)*	-5.2
Net contribution	**8.3**
CONTEXT	
Net contribution per person	£130
Net contribution/GDP	0.53%
Net contribution/UK public spending	1.20%

* Mainly for agriculture and regional policy
Figures for 2013/14

Britain is now one of the EU's richer nations. Our GDP per head was 10% above the EU average in 2012. That made us slightly richer than France but poorer than Germany. One reason we have shot up the rankings is because the club has been expanded over the past 40 years to include poorer countries in southern Europe (such as Greece and Portugal) and in eastern Europe (such as Poland and Hungary). These poorer countries are net beneficiaries of the EU budget.

We were very keen on this expansion – and rightly so. Thatcher, for example, saw that we could draw the former

Warsaw Pact countries out of Russia's sphere of influence and reinforce their transition to democracy if we invited them into the EU.

Our net contribution per head was 14% less than what Germany paid in 2011 and 17% more than what France pays[41]. We are still paying a bit more than we should compared to France and it would be good to cut the overall budget further. But our share of total expenditure is broadly fair.

CAPPING the damage

The ugliest EU policy is the CAP and associated policies for rural development. Not only does it absorb 39% of the EU's budget. It is also responsible for keeping food prices higher than they would otherwise be.

Mind you, even the CAP isn't nearly as ugly as it used to be. When Britain joined the then EEC in 1973, agriculture accounted for over three quarters of an admittedly far smaller budget. What's more, the CAP didn't just keep food prices high. The way it did this was by buying up lots of agricultural products at artificially high prices and then storing them. Hence, the grotesque wine lakes and butter mountains of the 1980s. Now that the Commission no longer buys up products and stores them, these have vanished.

The main purpose of today's CAP is to support rural incomes. Other goals are to ensure the EU has enough food to feed itself and to protect the environment. Though these are legitimate objectives, the CAP goes about achieving them in an inefficient way.

The first problem is that the CAP gives hand-outs which depend largely on the size of farms. This means that the biggest grants are typically given to the richest farmers, such as the Queen. One can argue that some of this money will trickle down to poor farm labourers. But the system is an indirect way of helping workers who, in any case, are already protected by the minimum wage.

The CAP does help the rural environment. But only 14% of the UK's subsidies are directed to green objectives such as biodiversity, so it is only helping a bit[42]. One might also ask why farmers need to be bribed to protect the environment. Other industries are told what to do to keep the environment clean and then fined, or otherwise punished, if they don't.

Finally, the EU's tariffs on imported agricultural produce, which range from 18%-28%, inflate prices. This costs British consumers 3.67 billion (£3.1 billion) a year, or 0.2% of GDP, according to the OECD.

Ideally, the whole system would be scrapped. That, though, is not politically possible. Probably the best we can do is keep chipping away at the cost of the subsidies, direct as big a proportion of the spending as possible to the environment and push for external tariffs to be cut. The next opportunity to make progress could be in 2016 when the EU's seven-year budget has a mid-term review.

If we quit the EU, we wouldn't be bound by the CAP. But things might not be a lot better. Our own farming lobby is strong, so the government would be under pressure to put in place some new agricultural policy that continued subsidising farmers. The cost might be lower than what we now pay but perhaps not by a lot.

What's more, the single market would be partly shut for our exports – unless we did a special deal with the EU. This is because our farmers would have to pay the EU's high agricultural tariffs. Dairy exports would incur especially punitive taxes of 55%, according to *The Economist*[43]. Cheddar cheese would face a tariff of 167/100 kilograms; while the mark-up on Stilton would be 141.

Our farmers' exports to the Continent would also still have to conform to EU food regulations. Meanwhile, we would have to decide whether to allow EU farm products unfettered access to the UK. If we did that without a reciprocal deal, our farmers would scream blue murder. So quitting the EU wouldn't be a complete solution for even the ugliest of its policies.

A fishy tale

If this book had been written a year earlier, the Common Fisheries Policy (CFP) would have taken top billing with the CAP in the ugly policy parade. The CFP was agreed by the original six members of the EEC just before we joined in 1973 and foisted upon us as part of the deal to sign up for membership. Edward Heath, our prime minister, was so desperate to join that he didn't put up a fight.

The CFP opened up our rich waters to fishermen from other countries. It wasn't a free-for-all as each nation was given quotas for how much they were allowed to catch of each type of fish in each of the main fishing basins – the North Sea, the Mediterranean and so forth. The overall quotas were supposed to be determined by scientific studies saying how much could be sustainably fished.

The CFP suffered two big defects. First, the quotas were almost always set too high. That meant nearly half of Atlantic stocks were overfished, according to the Commission. Second, when fishermen caught more than their quota of a particular fish, they just threw the often-dead animals back in the sea. Such discards reached nearly a quarter of total catches. These disastrous practices have denuded the sea of fish and pushed up prices in the process.

Fortunately, the EU agreed a revamp of the policy in 2013. Discards are virtually forbidden. What's more, the

Commission now only sets the general framework and overall targets. The UK and other fishing nations decide how to implement the policy, collaborating with each other as necessary. The moral of this tale is that even the ugliest of EU policies can be reformed.

Totally NUTS

Britain can largely blame France for the CAP. It has itself to blame for the EU's other big-spending programme: its regional policy. Two years after we joined the then EEC in 1973, we persuaded the other nations to give money to the Community's poorer regions. At the time, we were one of the poorer nations, behind Germany, France, Denmark and the Benelux countries, and what we got out of the regional policy helped even out what we lost under the CAP. Now we are one of the richer nations, mainly because other poorer countries have joined the EU, and so we lose out on this policy too.

The EU's main regional projects are building roads, ports, airports, bridges and other infrastructure. That's why, if you travel around southern or eastern Europe, you often see the EU's "flag" with its 12 stars on a blue background, proudly proclaiming what it is doing to help the local community. The biggest beneficiaries in absolute terms are Poland and Spain. On a per capita basis, the top 10 winners are all in central and eastern Europe, apart from Greece and Portugal.

The EU also gives money to poor regions in rich countries such as Germany, France and Britain. In the UK, two regions are considered particularly poor – Cornwall and west Wales. Just for good measure, a bit of cash is sprinkled over richer regions too. In euro-jargon, regions are called NUTS – or the Nomenclature of Territorial Units for Statistics. The amount of cash that goes to the NUTS is thrashed out as part of each seven-year budget round.

The policy's goal is to help poorer regions catch up with the rest. The idea is not bad in theory. When Greece, Spain and Portugal joined the then EEC in the 1980s after periods of being ruled by right-wing dictatorships, it made sense to entrench democracy by helping them kick-start their economies. Ditto for the eastern European countries who joined the EU after the Berlin Wall fell and they liberated themselves from Russian-imposed communism.

But the risk is that these programmes are a permanent subsidy to poorer regions rather than a time-limited bridge to help them deal with the transition to democracy and market economies. What's more, they are not limited to regions in countries transitioning to democracy. Sicily, for example, is a big beneficiary – as is Greece, 40 years after its military dictatorship fell.

Although NUTS grants do seem to have helped the regions a bit, centralised hand-outs are not the best way of promoting growth. There are only so many roads and bridges that it's sensible to build.

Take Portugal. A quarter of the 96 billion (£81 billion) it has received in regional grants since 1986 has been spent on roads, according to the *Financial Times*. It now has a glut – with four times as many motorway miles per inhabitant as Britain. Meanwhile, the EU Court of Auditors calculated in 2013 that the cost of building EU-financed roads in Spain was 73% more than building them in Germany. It couldn't explain why.

What's more, the allocation of funds is not performance-linked. Regions just get money if they comply with the regulations rather than if they improve efficiency[44]. Sometimes the funds are also abused or, at least, not properly accounted for. Indeed, that's the main reason that the Court of Auditors hasn't given the EU budget a clean bill of health for years.

We should advocate two changes. First, the European Commission should crack down harder on fraud and bad accounting. It does try to stop irregularities. In mid-2013, for example, Brussels temporarily suspended some payments to Hungary after it discovered deficiencies in the control systems of existing programmes. But it could be tougher. Why not institute a system whereby, for every euro that is misspent in a country in a year, a euro is deducted from the regional grants it receives the following year? That would give national governments an incentive to help root out bad practices.

Second, the EU's regional policy should be restricted to poor countries and the money-go-round where cash is sent from richer countries to Brussels and back again should be stopped. If grants were only given to countries whose GDP/head was less than 90% of the EU average, Britain's gross contribution to the budget would have been 15.2 billion (£12.8 billion) less during 2007-2013, according to Open Europe. We might, of course, have decided to spend most of the cash we saved on our own regional policy. But that would be our choice and we could spend the money as we wished.

Such a repatriation of regional policy to richer countries wouldn't require any treaty changes. But it would need unanimous agreement by governments during the budget negotiations. The last Labour government advocated such a policy. But the coalition didn't push it during the 2014-2020 budget round. Whoever is in government in 2016, though, should put this on the agenda for the mid-term budget review.

If we left the EU, we wouldn't have to subsidise other EU countries' poorer regions, would we? Well, not so fast. That depends on the sort of deal that we cut after we left. If Britain pulled out of the single market too, we might get away without paying anything into the EU kitty. But, as previously mentioned, if we copied Norway – which is in the single market but not the EU – we would have to contribute to the EU's regional policy, albeit not as much as we do now. In other words, we'd end up paying alimony.

Social dumping myth

John Major secured an opt-out from the Social Chapter when he signed the Maastricht Treaty in 1992. Tony Blair threw it away as soon as he got into office in 1997. He had every right to pass laws copying the legislation contained in the Social Chapter. But, by signing a treaty, he committed the UK to these policies in a way that makes it hard to wriggle out of them. We would either have to persuade all the other 27 countries to agree to give us back our opt-out in a new treaty or quit the EU entirely.

The EU has the power to make policy over a wide range of social and employment issues. The main areas are gender equality, health and safety at work, working conditions, social security and industrial relations. The UK certainly needs laws on these matters; and most of what Brussels has decided – with a few glaring exceptions such as the Working Time Directive and health and safety legislation – hasn't been too costly. But why should the EU be meddling in these things at all? These are precisely the sorts of decisions that ought to be left to national governments, under the "subsidiarity principle".

Unfortunately, many continental Europeans, led by the French, believe that if the UK was free to operate within the single market without abiding by minimum social regulations, our companies would have an unfair advantage. Countries across the Channel would either lose jobs or have to follow suit, leading to a race to the bottom in the provision of social protection. The French often use the term "social dumping" to describe the process by which countries with weak social regulations can dump cheap products in countries with strong rules.

Social dumping is a rogue argument, designed to protect out-of-date and unsustainable welfare states in places like France. While there are some advantages in a high level of social protection, it comes with a cost – both to business and taxpayers.

Countries should be free to decide where to strike the balance. Rich ones may well opt for a higher level of protection because they want it and can afford it. But forcing all EU countries to have a high level of protection would harm the ability of the weaker ones to compete with companies from countries in the rest of the world such as America and China. The EU should actually welcome rivalry between Europe's social systems as that would spur the weaker countries to reform their practices and so get fit enough to compete in the rest of the world.

Getting back our opt-out from social policy is probably impossible. Instead we should adopt a twin-track policy of reforming the most onerous existing rules and stopping any bad new ones. We also need to accept that we can't decide other countries' red lines for them. The French will not drop the social dumping argument just because we say it doesn't make sense.

With existing rules, the priorities are the Working Time Directive and the Temporary Agency Workers Directive (TAWD), which guarantees those who work via employment agencies the same pay and conditions as people who work as employees.

We may be able to make some progress on our own. For example, the Institute of Directors has argued that we could save UK business £1.2 billion a year if we let firms that decide employment terms through individual rather than collective negotiations opt out of the TAWD. We'll also need to work with allies – for example, to change the definition of "on call time" in the Working Time Directive so that when workers are asleep at their workplace that doesn't count towards their maximum working hours.

As for stopping new rules, one option would be to get an "emergency brake", allowing any government to veto new legislation that affected fundamental aspects of its social or employment systems. Countries wanting new rules would be free to press ahead, but the others wouldn't be forced to.

The EU already has a precedent for such an emergency brake in social security and criminal justice, as previously mentioned. If the treaties are reopened, the UK should argue that it is extended to social policy in general on the grounds that light-touch regulation is necessary to boost the EU's competitiveness and that, in any case, such matters should be left to national governments. Part of the advantage of taking this line is that we could claim that we were doing something for the whole of the EU, not asking for a special deal for Britain.

Welfare tourism

A common complaint about Brussels is that it forces us to open our doors to EU immigrants, who then come here and live off benefits. As argued previously, the overwhelming majority of EU immigrants come here to work and, in the process, pay taxes. A higher proportion of them are in employment and a lower percentage on benefits than the native population. They are contributing to the vibrancy of our economy. We get a good financial deal from welcoming hard-working migrants from across the Channel.

Even if one accepts that the lion's share of EU immigrants come here to work, aren't there a few "welfare tourists" that deliberately come here to take advantage of unemployment benefit, child benefit, the NHS and so forth? The answer is that there are very few of them. Why would people uproot themselves to cross Europe to come to a country where benefits aren't that generous in the first place? If they really wanted to become welfare tourists, they would be better off going to Germany or Scandinavia.

The facts bear out this thesis. Only 0.2% of EU immigrants – that's around 5,000 people in total – claim unemployment benefit without ever having worked in the UK, according to the Centre for European Reform[7]. Many of these probably aren't even welfare tourists as they could have come here with the hope of finding a job and not succeeded.

EU immigrants aren't coming to the UK for child benefit or tax credits either. Only 2.1% and 1% respectively claim child benefit or tax credits within a year of arriving here. By comparison, one-fifth of the British working-age population claim these benefits.

So "welfare tourism" isn't a big economic problem. But it is a political problem. As a result, the coalition has been tightening up the rules since late 2013: new migrants will have to wait for three months before qualifying for unemployment benefit; payments will be stopped after three months unless the claimant has a genuine chance of getting a job; and new migrants won't be able to get housing benefit immediately. This was right at the limit of what we could do without infringing EU law – and there's even a chance that Brussels will argue that we have breached it.

The Tories would like to go further. This would have to involve changing EU law – which will probably happen given that other governments, including Germany, are worried about benefit abuses. There's also strong popular support for restricting the rights of immigrants to benefits: 61% of Brits think they should wait at least three years before they can get benefits[1].

But we shouldn't kid ourselves that there's much, if any, money to be made from changing EU law to make it harder for non-citizens to access welfare states. After all, there are 2.2 million Brits living in the rest of the EU – and what's sauce for the goose is sauce for the gander.

There are, for example, about 40,000 Brits on unemployment benefit in the rest of the EU, according to the *Sunday Times*. That compares with 38,000 EU nationals who were on the dole here in 2011, according to official statistics[45]. What's more, benefits on the other side of the Channel are often more generous than in the UK. In Germany, some Brits are raking in up to £23,318 a year in unemployment benefit, according to the *Sunday Times* – much more than they'd get for being on the dole at home.

No comprehensive study has been done comparing how much we spend on welfare for EU citizens with how much other EU countries spend on welfare for British citizens. But it wouldn't be surprising if we gain more on the swings than we lose on the roundabouts.

Climatology

Some environmental issues such as global warming and acid rain cross national boundaries; others such as the cleanliness of drinking and bathing water don't. In environmental policy, the subsidiarity test is important: decisions about the former should be taken by the EU or at a global level;

decisions about the latter should be taken by nation states. This is not a call for Britain to have dirty drinking water or polluted beaches. But if that's really what the people want, it should be their right to choose it.

The EU doesn't always draw the line in the right place. The Dutch government, for example, has argued that Brussels should only concern itself with the flood risks of cross-border rivers. But this is small beer compared to global warming. Unless you are a climate change denier, it is clear we need to take action at a global level. Agreeing a policy at a EU level and seeking to use its clout to press for a global deal is a good place to start.

Not that the EU has got its global warming policy quite right. One of its key targets is that 20% of all energy should be produced by renewable technologies by 2020. The UK's target is actually slightly less – 15%. But we were starting from an extremely low base of 1.3% in 2005, so this is a challenging target which the government has estimated will cost £66 billion over 20 years[46].

A renewable target is an inefficient way of achieving the objective of cutting greenhouse gas emissions. It may be cheaper, for example, to use nuclear power or invest in energy conservation. The EU should, therefore, set targets for cutting emissions while leaving countries to decide the best way of hitting them. Fortunately, as of early 2014, it looked like this would be the EU's approach for hitting the targets that will be set for 2030.

The other main limb of the EU's global warming policy is a "cap-and-trade" scheme. This involves setting a "cap" on how much carbon dioxide energy companies and large industrial enterprises are allowed to spew out into the atmosphere every year. By 2020, the overall cap will be 21% less than it was in 2005. Quotas are auctioned off or given to individual companies, which are then free to trade the quotas among themselves. The idea is that those who can cut their emissions most cheaply will sell their quotas to those which have to spend a lot to curb pollution – and, as a result, the cost to the economy of fighting global warming will be minimised.

The EU's cap-and-trade scheme alone won't stop global warming. That's partly because factory and power station emissions are only responsible for about half the bloc's carbon pollution. Cars, lorries, agriculture and buildings are responsible for the rest.

Some critics also argue that the scheme isn't working because emissions fell during the post-credit crunch recession and, as a result, so did the carbon price. But this isn't a good criticism. The overall cap is still coming down by 21% by 2020. If this can be done more cheaply because of the recession, at least the financial crisis has had one silver lining.

More important, the EU is only responsible for 11% of global emissions. Global warming is a classic case of a problem that requires a global solution – and that is proving difficult. A treaty called the Kyoto protocol was agreed in 1997. But America, the world's second-largest carbon polluter, refused to ratify it. What's more, although the protocol set targets for developed nations to cut their emissions, it did not do so for developing nations. This is a big omission given that China is now the largest source of carbon emissions and India the third largest.

That said, by acting together with the other 27 EU nations, Britain has a better chance of persuading China and America to agree a global deal than it would if it was on its own. And if they don't, we will also have more options of stopping what could then legitimately be called environmental dumping.

The EU has already taken a step in this direction with its plan to charge foreign airlines for their carbon emissions over EU airspace. A more dramatic policy would be to impose an import tax on goods and services from countries that don't do their fair share to curb carbon emissions. Such a move could cause a trade war and so should only be adopted when all possibility of dialogue had been exhausted. But if Britain quit the EU, we wouldn't even be able to dream of taking such action.

War-war

If you think foreign policy is about fighting wars, the EU hasn't achieved much. It failed to intervene militarily in the Bosnian War in the 1990s, even when 8,000 men were massacred in Srebrenica. It was only after Nato took action that the war came to an end – although, after that, the EU did send peace envoys and peacekeeping troops.

Meanwhile, when America decided to invade Iraq to bring down Saddam Hussein, the EU was hopelessly divided. Among the big nations, Britain, Italy and Spain joined the campaign, while Germany and France were opposed. More recently, Britain and France were able to agree on a campaign to bring down Libya's Colonel Gaddafi. But there was no EU approach – not least because Germany abstained on a vote to authorise a no-fly zone in the United Nations Security Council. The EU has also been all over the shop on what to do in Syria.

Since 1949, the bulwark of Europe's defence has been the trans-Atlantic relationship with America via Nato. We are members and so are almost all other EU countries including former Warsaw Pact states such as Poland. So are a few non-EU countries, the most important of which is Turkey. Whenever a complex military operation is required, it is necessary to bring in Nato and America.

The EU is not capable of heavy lifting, but it can help with what are effectively glorified police and training operations. In mid-2013, it had four military missions in the field: peace-keeping in Bosnia, anti-piracy off the coast of Somalia and training for Mali and Somalia. The total annual cost of these military missions was projected at 52 million (£44 million), of which Britain's share was 8 million (£7 million)[47]. Just over 100 of our military personnel were involved.

The EU at present achieves little in the field of military action partly because unanimity is required and it is rare that all 28 countries will agree. What's more, many countries, including Britain, are not yet ready to give up their vetoes over foreign and defence policy.

That said, the EU's small operations could be the kernel of something more important. There is also scope for European countries to work together to get better value for the weapons we buy. Indeed, in a summit in late 2013, leaders agreed to cooperate on developing drones, air-to-air refuelling equipment and cyber defence systems.

The need to do this will grow as America continues its "pivot" away from Europe and towards China and, as a result, Nato gets hollowed out. This is not something we should encourage. But we cannot control global events. As America reduces its commitment to European defence, we will have to step up cooperation with our EU allies. That will be much harder if we quit the EU.

Jaw-jaw

Foreign policy is not just about fighting wars. It is mainly about using our influence to promote our interests in non-violent ways. The EU has three main tools for doing this: trade, aid and sanctions. The carrot of trading with a rich bloc with over 500 million people is the most powerful. It gives us influence on matters such as prying open foreign markets, stitching together deals to stop multinational companies evade tax and pushing for action to stop global warming. Aid is a useful extra carrot for inducing poorer countries to follow policies we like. Meanwhile, sanctions – such as those imposed on Russia in 2014 after its annexation of Crimea – can be a worthwhile stick. All these tools are much more effective if the EU acts together than if the UK acted alone.

In 2012, the EU received the Nobel Peace Prize for contributing to the advancement of peace, reconciliation, democracy and human rights within Europe. We shouldn't believe the hyperbole of some euro-enthusiasts to the effect that the EU was responsible for this single-handedly. Hitler's Germany was so roundly defeated that it wasn't likely that it was going to launch a Third World War anyway. Nevertheless, the creation of the then EEC did bind Germany's and France's economies together in such a way that war between the two is now unthinkable. Moreover, they now have a largely friendly relationship – as, indeed, we do with our own erstwhile enemy Germany.

The EU can also take only limited credit for winning the Cold War. America and Nato – and, of course, the people of eastern Europe – deserve the main accolades. But the EU, and especially Britain under Thatcher, can get plaudits for institutionalising democracy and free markets in the newly liberated countries of eastern Europe after the Berlin Wall fell. In return for joining the EU, countries that were formerly part of the Soviet empire had to entrench human rights, the rule of law, democracy and a broadly market economy.

The lure of EU membership was first used to embed democracy in Greece, Spain and Portugal after their right-wing dictatorships fell. It is now being used in the Balkans. Slovenia and Croatia have already joined. Serbia, Bosnia, Montenegro, Albania, Kosovo and the Former Yugoslav Republic of Macedonia are candidates or potential candidates. It would have been far better if Yugoslavia hadn't torn itself apart in bloodshed. But the fact that the fragments of the old Yugoslavia are joining the EU makes the prospect of another Balkan war virtually impossible.

What, though, has all this got to do with whether Britain should stay in the EU? We weren't part of the EEC when France and Germany first decided to bury the hatchet and they are hardly going to go back to war if we quit. And, while the UK under Margaret Thatcher played a big role in pressing the EU to expand to the East, Poland isn't going to re-join the Warsaw Pact if we are no longer an EU member.

All this is true. However, there are yet more prizes to be had in expanding the frontiers of freedom in Europe.

The EU acted as a beacon of prosperity and peace for the 2014 Ukrainian revolution. When the regime of Viktor Yanukovich turned its back on an EU free trade deal and, instead, nuzzled up to Russia's Vladimir Putin, his people rebelled. Europe now needs to help Ukraine, with its 46 million people, become a free, democratic and successful country. This should include holding out the promise that it can become an EU member in the long run.

Eurospectics may worry about the prospect of a flood of new immigrants from the east. But we should remember that immigration from eastern Europe is largely positive for our economy as those who come here are young, hard-working and pay taxes. Remember, too, that geopolitics isn't just about economics. Securing democracy in our neighbourhood is good for humanity and our own long-term security.

If Ukraine can make the transition to freedom, even Russia may follow suit.

It won't be easy to bring the Ukraine crisis to a satisfactory conclusion. The country is bankrupt, corruption is rife and Putin is trying to destabilise it. In order to help, the EU will need to focus on the problems for many years and it's not clear it has the ability to do this. That said, in early 2014, there were positive signs that the main EU nations, including the UK, were forming a common position on how to manage the situation. Putin had given the EU a purpose in foreign policy that it had lacked for years. Neither Britain nor the rest of the EU would have as good a chance of being effective on its own.

There is a similar opportunity in Turkey. When the mostly young protestors occupied Taksim Square in 2013, they were motivated by the conviction that Turkey should become a modern European country. The crackdown by Prime Minister Tayyip Erdogan shows that the country is still a long way from qualifying for EU membership. But if Turkey does take a decisive step towards democracy, the EU should respond.

The UK has long been keen on Turkey, with its 77 million people, joining the EU. This is partly because it would be good for trade and partly because a strongly pro-Western Turkey could be a good role model for the Middle East. France and Germany have been much more reluctant, fearing an influx of Muslim immigrants. If we quit the EU, there will be less chance of bringing Turkey into the fold.

Even where the lure of EU membership is not realistic, we could and should play an active role in promoting peace, democracy and human rights in our near neighbourhood: North Africa and the Middle East. Since the Suez crisis in 1956, we have often played the role of America's junior partner in the Middle East. The results have been disastrous. Not only was Britain sucked into the invasion of Iraq, Israel has not made peace with the Palestinians and much of the rest of the Middle East is riven with strife and civil war.

America would like to downgrade its involvement in the Middle East – partly because of the trauma of Iraq and partly because, following the shale gas boom, it isn't desperate for Persian Gulf oil to fuel its gas-guzzling economy. In many ways, less activism by America would be a good thing. But it also means there could be a power vacuum on the southern coast of the Mediterranean which, among other things, is fuelling a wave of illegal immigrants some of whom tragically end up dying on the high seas.

We are further away from the hot spots than other EU countries such as Italy. But this is still our back yard and it's in our interest that it is as peaceful as possible. If America retreats, we have no chance of conducting an effective Middle Eastern foreign policy alone. Collaboration with the EU will be the best solution.

Looking to the future, it will be increasingly in our interests to make common cause with our EU partners. Whether we are fending off bullying from Russia, helping to sort out the mess in the Middle East or negotiating trade deals with China, clout matters. We will need to develop a more effective EU foreign policy over the coming years. But we won't be able to play any role in it if we quit. Both our power and that of the rest of the EU will be diminished.

Chapter Eight
The Balance Sheet

How should we weigh up the pros and cons of EU membership? First look at the advantages and disadvantages as things stand; then examine the opportunities to maximise the positives and minimise the negatives; finally consider the break-up costs. We can't quantify all these elements. But even though we should treat all guesstimates as indicating only the rough ballpark, we can still draw a clear conclusion.

Start with things as they stand. Access to the single market, and the common market before it, has boosted GDP by around 4-5%[48]. That's not the same as saying we'd lose 4-5% of GDP if we quit, but it gives a rough idea of the magnitude.

There are also three other substantial advantages of membership: clout in trade talks, free movement of people and influence in foreign policy. These are harder to quantify. It is not even worth trying to putting a figure on foreign policy. But, as other countries such as China get more powerful, the ability to make a bigger impact by clubbing together with our neighbours will become increasingly valuable.

Now look at the main tangible costs of membership: our net budget contribution and the way the Common Agricultural Policy pushes up food prices. These cost us 0.5% and 0.2% of GDP respectively – or 0.7% of GDP in total.

So if we just look at things as they stand, the quantifiable benefits clearly outweigh the costs. That's before taking account of benefits such as free movement of people and clout, and the cost of unnecessary red tape.

We should add to this the opportunities for maximising the positives and minimising the negatives. The zeitgeist in Europe is changing. Growing euroscepticism and a greater appreciation of the importance of competitiveness mean we have a golden opportunity to push for reforms.

There are three big ones: completing the single market; cutting ambitious free trade deals with the US and Japan; and enhancing the City as Europe's financial centre. The first two have been quantified at up to 8.1% of GDP[49] and 1.3% of GDP respectively – or 9.4% of GDP in total. No work has been done on enhancing the City as a financial centre. But the benefits would be substantial. We couldn't get these if we quit.

Balance sheet on EU membership

PROS	CONS
Single market - 4-5% of GDP	CAP inflates food prices - 0.2% of GDP
Clout in trade talks	Budget - net cost 0.5% of GDP
Free movement of people	Extra red tape
Clout in foreign policy	Meddling by Brussels
No hefty break-up costs	

OPPORTUNITIES

TO MAXIMISE PROS	TO MINIMISE CONS
Complete single market - 7.1% of GDP	Reform onerous social legislation
Implement single market rules - 1% of GDP	Let rich countries run own regional policy
Enhance City as Europe's financial centre	Cut red tape
Free trade deals with US/Japan - 1.3% of GDP	Cut farm subsidies
	Greater powers for national parliaments and emergency brake for social rules if treaties reopened

One thing to notice about these numbers is that, even if we get only half of the benefits, they would dwarf the costs of EU membership. Meanwhile, the changing zeitgeist also gives us a chance to minimise the intangible costs: to reform onerous rules, let richer countries such as the UK run their own regional policies and cut farm subsidies. If the EU treaties are reopened, we may be also able to secure changes that prevent meddling by Brussels, such as greater powers for national parliaments and an emergency brake for social rules. And, of course, we always have an opportunity to remove the gold plate we've layered on top of EU laws.

Remember how none of the alternatives to EU membership is good and how exiting would create years of uncertainty, because a "no" vote wouldn't clarify which type of "out" the people wanted. There would be a period of internal wrangling, followed by negotiations with our EU partners. In some circumstances, these could turn acrimonious. While it's hard to predict how all this will turn out, one thing is clear: business dislikes uncertainty. During the divorce negotiations, the economy would suffer.

Demographics is destiny

We should also lift our eyes a bit to the horizon. Many eurosceptics view the EU as a foreign conspiracy foisted upon us, in which we are condemned always to play a defensive role in a vain attempt to minimise the damage caused by French and German machinations.

While we certainly lost out by not joining the common market at the outset – and have had to contend with the wasteful Common Agricultural Policy as a result – this is an extremely one-sided version of history. Britain has played a decisive role in creating the single market, expanding the EU to the east and in pushing for free trade with the rest of the world. English is also the working language of the EU, as well as the lingua franca of Europe's younger generation.

In 2014, it is easy to suppose that Europe will always be dominated by Germany. It, after all, has a population of 82 million versus Britain's 63 million. And its GDP per head is higher – in part because the single market in manufacturing plays to its strengths.

But fast forward to 2050. By then, Britain's population will have grown to 71 million and Germany's will have shrunk to 68 million, according to the World Bank. We could have the largest population in the EU, assuming Scotland doesn't vote for independence. This is partly because of immigration, but also because our people are more fertile than Germans and most other Europeans.

Our population will also be younger. We will have 12 million children aged less than 15, compared to only 9 million in Germany. We will also have fewer old people: 18 million aged 65 or above, compared with 22 million in Germany. Meanwhile, in the prime working age of 15-64, there will be more Brits: 42 million versus 37 million.

Britain also has strengths in many of the industries of the future: finance, creative industries, education and other services. In many of these, the English language is a great advantage. If we can complete the single market in services, our services companies will enjoy the same sort of economies of scale that benefit German manufacturers today.

By 2050, Britain could well have not just the largest population in the EU, but the largest economy too. That's certainly what Goldman Sachs is predicting[50]. As a result, we are well placed to provide joint leadership of the EU alongside the Germans and French in the years to come – provided, of course, we don't quit.

Our EU membership is valuable, we can make it even better and the break-up costs could be large. We are better off in than out.

Euro Jargon

CAP (Common Agricultural Policy)
The EU's agricultural policy and its largest spending programme.

Council of Ministers
The EU body where ministers from the 28 countries gather to approve legislation proposed by the European Commission (see below). Most decisions are taken by qualified majority voting (see below).

Directive
The main form of EU law. Directives are proposed by the European Commission and approved by both the Council of Ministers and the European Parliament. They are then translated into national laws.

ECB (European Central Bank)
The euro zone's central bank. It does not have authority over Britain.

ECJ (European Court of Justice)
The EU's supreme court. If there are disputes over the functioning of the EU, it determines who is wrong and can punish the miscreants.

EEA (European Economic Area)
A group of 31 countries, including all the EU members and all of the EFTA members with the exception of Switzerland. The EEA members have a single market for good and services.

EEC (European Economic Community)
The EU's original name. It was renamed after the Maastricht Treaty.

EFTA (European Free Trade Association)
A group of four European countries – Iceland, Liechtenstein, Norway and Switzerland – which often negotiate free trade deals as a bloc. Britain was part of EFTA until it joined the EU. All the EFTA countries, with the exception of Switzerland, are part of the EEA.

EU (European Union)
A group of 28 countries which have agreed a set of treaties about how they will act together in various areas including trade, agriculture, the environment, social policy and home affairs.

Euro zone
The 18 EU countries that have decided to use the euro. Britain is not part of the euro zone.

European Commission
The EU institution which proposes new laws and implements existing ones. Commissioners are proposed by the European Council and approved by the European Parliament.

European Council
The EU body where leaders of the 28 countries meet. It sets the EU's overall direction and priorities.

European Parliament
The EU institution made up of MEPs (see below). Along with the Council of Ministers, it approves legislation proposed by the European Commission.

MEPs
Members of the European Parliament. They are directly elected by the people in each of the 28 member countries every five years.

Non-tariff barriers
Rules and practices that make it hard for goods and services to be sold across national frontiers. The EU made a big push to remove non-tariff barriers in 1992, but many still remain – especially in services. Non-tariff barriers are common between the EU and the rest of the world.

QMV (qualified majority voting)
The main form of voting in the Council of Ministers. From November 2014, at least 55% of countries, representing at least 65% of the EU's population, are needed to approve laws. Britain accounts for 12.5% of the EU's population.

Social Chapter
A protocol on social policy attached to the Maastricht Treaty, which didn't originally apply to Britain. It was included in the Amsterdam Treaty and now applies to Britain too.

Subsidiarity principle
The principle under which the EU is only supposed to take action if it can do so more effectively than a nation state can alone.

Tariff barriers
Taxes on imports. All tariff barriers within the then EEC were removed in 1968. But tariff barriers still exist between the EU and much of the rest of the world.

Temporary Agency Workers Directive
An EU law guaranteeing those who work via employment agencies the same pay and conditions as people who work as employees.

Working Time Directive
An EU law which, among other things, stops people working more than 48 hours a week. Britain has an opt-out from the key provision and, as a result, anybody is free to work more than 48 hours a week but nobody can be forced to do so.

Footnotes

1. British Social Attitudes Survey 2014

2. Parliamentary Business, Parliament UK – Britons Living and Working Abroad, February, 2014

3. Migrant entrepreneurs: building our businesses, creating our jobs, Centre for Entrepreneurs in 2104

4. Centre for Research and Analysis of Migration, UCL: The fiscal Effects of Immigration to the UK, 2013. These statistics refer to EEA immigrants (EU plus Norway, Iceland and Liechtenstein).

5. Centre for Economics and Business Research: The impact of the European Union on the UK labour market, 2013

6. Migration Advisory Committee: Migrants in low-skilled work, 2014

7. Centre for European Reform: Is immigration a reason for Britain to leave the EU? 2013

8. Romanians use cheap flights for crime spree, *The Times*, October 2, 2013

9. UKIP Manifesto, 2014

10. Criminal Justice Statistics Quarterly, December 2013

11. UK government - Review of balance of competences: Free movement of persons, 2014

12. European Council Communiqué, June 2014

13. For a more detailed examination of the options look at: Open Europe – Trading Places – Is EU membership still the best option for UK trade? 2012

14. Letter from Australian foreign minister to British foreign minister 2013

15. The UK Automotive Industry and the EU, KPMG 2014

16. Doing things by halves: Alternatives to UK EU membership, CBI, 2013

17. HM Treasury: EU Membership and Trade

18. Strategic directions for Switzerland's financial market policy, 2009

19. David Buchan, Centre for European Reform – Outsiders on the inside: Swiss and Norwegian lessons for the UK, 2012

20. China Tax Alert, KPMG, July 2013 – Is the China-Switzerland Free Trade Agreement for you?

21. The City UK – UK and the EU: A mutually beneficial relationship, 2013

22. Interview with FAZ

23. Report by PwC for City of London Corporation

24. Centre for Economic Policy Research – estimating the economic impact on the UK of a transatlantic trade and investment partnership agreement between the European Union and the United States, 2013

25. How much legislation comes from Europe? House of Commons Library, October 2010

26. Actually, there are lots of Councils – one for different policy areas such as economics, foreign affairs and agriculture. Just to make things even more confusing, there is a body called the Council of Europe. This is nothing to do with the EU.

27. Cited by Katinka Barysch in Tilting at European Windmills, Centre for European Reform, 2013

28. Why Europe needs cross-border lawnmower regulations, *Financial Times* October 15, 2013

29. Open Europe – Top 100 list, 2013

30. For an excellent analysis of this directive, see CER: The Working Time Directive, What's the fuss about? Katinka Barysch, 2013

31. See Business for New Europe: The Single Market – Filling the Gaps, 2013 (unpublished)

32. Letter from Michel Barnier, 2013 (unpublished)

33. Centre for European Reform: How to build a modern European Union, 2013

34. See Open Europe: Kick-starting growth: How to reignite the EU's services sector, 2013

35. A good summary of the evidence is contained in this government report: Review of the Balance of Competences between the united Kingdom and the European Union: The Single Market, July 2013

36. Boltho, A. & B. Eichengreen (2008) – The Economic Impact of European Integration (CEPR Discussion Paper No. 6820)

37. CBI: Our Global future: business vision for a reformed EU, 2013

38. Brexit or Fixit? The Trade and Welfare Effects of Leaving the European Union, LSE's Centre for Economic Performance, May 2014

39. The economic consequences for the UK and the EU of completing the Single Market, BIS, 2011

40. HM Treasury European Union Finances, 2012

41. Calculations based on European Commission: EU budget 2011

42. Open Europe – More for less: Making the EU's farm policy work for growth and the environment, 2012

43. Making the break, *The Economist*, December 8, 2012

44. Open Europe – Off Target: The case for bringing regional policy back home, 2012

45. Quoted in a European Commission report on benefit tourism, 2013

46. Open Europe: Submission to the balance of competences review: environment and climate change, 2013

47. UK government – Review of the balance of competences: Foreign policy report, 2013

48. The figures in this chapter on costs and benefits are explained in previous chapters

49. Including the benefits from implementing existing rules

50. Goldman Sachs: The BRICs 10 years on: halfway through the great transformation, 2011

Acknowledgments

Any flaws in this book are my responsibility. But the many people with whom I've discussed my views on Britain's relationship with Europe should share the credit. I would like to mention, in particular, my former colleagues at Reuters Breakingviews. I remember fondly the morning conferences when we debated the nuances of the euro crisis. Such collaborative intellectual reflection is an excellent way of clarifying both facts and opinions. Special thanks are due to Viktoria Dendrinou, who dug out many statistics for this book. I wish to thank my agent, Araminta Whitley, and her colleague Peta Nightingale – as well as Catherine Trevethan, who produced the graphics. I also am grateful to Thomson Reuters. Some passages in *The In Out Question* – especially *Let People Roam Free, Wounding the Golden Goose, Capital Idea, The Competitiveness Solution and Welfare Tourism* – are modifications of columns I wrote for Reuters as Editor-at-Large. I also wish to thank the *Financial Times* for letting me use some excerpts from a column I wrote in the *Capital Idea* section.

The following people read the manuscript: Jose Areilza, Charles Grant, John Grant, Edward Hadas, Edward Lucas, Gareth Penny, Kate Penny, Mats Persson, Roland Rudd, Laura Sandys, Phillip Souta, Will Tanner, Lucy Thomas,

Stephen Wall, Martin Wolf and Jan Zielonka. I thank them all for their comments.

Last but not least, I wish to thank to Isabelle Dupuy. She not only read the book and discussed the ideas in it, the first draft was written at her beach house in Haiti – an ideal place to gain perspective on Britain's relationship with Europe.

12671558R00077

Printed in Great Britain
by Amazon.co.uk, Ltd.,
Marston Gate.